TH

MARRIAGE

MANUAL

&

HANDBOOK

Practical Application to Proven Principles

But if in your fear you would seek only love's peace and love's pleasure,

Then it is better for you that you cover your nakedness and pass out of love's threshing-floor,

Into the seasonless world where you shall laugh, but not all of your laughter, and weep, but not all of your tears.

Kalil Gibran
Excerpt from "The Prophet"
1923

THE
MARRIAGE
MANUAL
&
HANDBOOK

Practical Application to Proven Principles

C. JOSEPH SIMPSON

This book was written as a guide and reference for those desiring an additional resource for the betterment of the understanding of their relationships. It is not intended to be used as an alternative to marital or family therapy or counseling. In fact, the author is a proponent of marital and family therapy and counseling. The author does not claim any responsibility or liability either directly or indirectly because of a perceived notion the reader may have grasped from reading this body of work.

Cover Design: Turner Studios, Joseph Turner

ISBN: **978-0-578-10734-9**

To Cynthia

Acknowledgements

We have been brought from whence we came through a series of life experiences and decisions. We have been brought to this very second of our lives because of our given path, our obedience, disobedience and the very people we have allowed in our lives to assist the potter in the shaping of the clay.

I am forever grateful to Almighty God for my very existence and for bestowing upon me gifts and talents. I acknowledge and understand that these gifts are not my own nor did I do anything of myself to achieve them or earn them. I am forever grateful and I pray I am not a disappointment.

I am forever thankful and indebted to my two late fathers, my biological father, Curley J. Simpson Sr. and my father-in-law, Leroy J. Welch. Even beyond the grave you gentlemen still amaze me. You are and have always been men amongst men. The more I mature, the wiser I see that you were when you were among us. A wise man once told me, "You never truly know how right your father is until you have a son telling you how wrong you are." I am truly beginning to understand.

I would like to thank my mother, Ella R. S. Daigle and my other father, Orell P. Daigle. It has truly been a pleasure to see you two young folks transition from good life to good life. Thank you so much for teaching me patience and grace not only in word but more importantly in deed.

To my mentors, Minister L.F.M. and Bishop R.B.P., you have assisted the potter immeasurably in shaping and molding the clay.

Because of you gentleman, I am not the same man that I was when I started my journey into manhood. As one taught me natural application, the other taught me spiritual implication. Once I married the two, all of the pieces of the puzzle that I acquired in life began to take shape and form. Life began to make sense once you taught me to apply wisdom to knowledge and understanding.

I am forever grateful to the Senior editor of this book, my beloved wife Cynthia, and our four children, Trey, Jabril, Josiah and Jealah, my God, what can I say? I truly want to thank you for your love, honor and support. You have made life so much easier than it could have been. Thank you for selflessly giving me enough time to study, write and produce this body of work. You are my inspiration and the very air I breathe. I love you with everything in me and Mrs. Simpson; I love you with *all of my foolish heart.*

I would also like to thank my friend and brother, Dr. Khalid Shabazz, one of the finest and most compassionate military chaplains I have ever met. Thank you for motivating and inciting me in pulling this work off of the shelf and completing it. I am forever grateful. To my editor, Mr. Patrick Farmer, who is responsible for many of the virtues yet none of the faults of this book, I would like to thank you for your tenacity, patience and soft nudges that you used to get me through this project.

I would lastly like to thank all of those who have allowed me into their relationships, lives and minds while this book was being developed. The knowledge I gained from you was some of the greatest acquired in pursuit of this workmanship. I pray this body of work meets your expectations and was worth your time.

C. Joseph Simpson

Contents

Preface

The book of Ecclesiastes is believed to be written by the wisest man to have ever lived, King Solomon. It's safe to say that much of his wisdom were his God given gifts and talents but if you ever read Ecclesiastes, you'll be able to see that much of his wisdom also came from his life experiences. If I were a betting man, I would also bet that not only did he learn from his own life experiences but he also learned from the life experiences of others. A wise man is one that *learns* from his experiences and puts those experiences into practice. The wisest of men however is one that not only learns from his experiences but also from the experiences of others. You don't have to hit your head on a brick wall to see how hard it actually is. No, I've seen too many people hit their heads and I know exactly how hard it is. I don't need bruises to prove it.

In my lifetime I've come to realize that I have been blessed with a gift of understanding people and relationships. My gifts and talents have afforded me the opportunity to mentor, educate, and counsel people on relationships as I made my way around the world at least 3 times. I've noticed that no matter what the age, color, nationality or sex, issues within relationships usually arise from poor foundational understandings. It's like when someone is ill and goes to the doctor. The doctor will be able to diagnose the illness because he knows that the person's body is not operating according to its basic and normal functions. It is the same way with diagnosing an ailing relationship. It's easy to see where there is a breakdown in the normal functions or basic foundations of the relationship.

I was speaking to a young woman a few years ago about some relationship issues that she was having. As I listened intently, I began to ask her questions. I then proceeded to guide her with more questions and then while she was in the middle of answering her own questions to her own problems she stopped and said, "Simp, you need to write a book! So many people don't know what you call basic." I really never gave what she said a second thought. I was simply trying to get her to see that what was going on in her life was repairable if she actually understood it.

As time went on and my children began to reach their preteens, it dawned on me that they were reaching the age I was when I lost my father. They were reaching the point where I began my painful period of trial and error. I didn't want them to have to go through the same distressing period of self discovery. If something were to befall me, I would want to leave them with something that would assist them in gaining a little piece of heaven on earth and that is, a peaceful and fulfilling relationship. I wanted to give them everything that I knew I would one day have to speak to them about but may not be here to do. I just sat down and began to type. Whatever thoughts came to my mind, I typed. I didn't have chapters, outlines or formats. I just typed everything I thought they would need to know. I then started to break my writings down into sections so it would be easier for them to find what they were looking for if they should be dealing with a particular issue.

Once I let a few people read a couple of sections to see if they thought I was on the right track and no matter which section they read, I'd always hear, "Man, this is awesome! I never thought about it like that. I was dealing with something and it makes sense to me now. You need to put this in a book!" I once read a quote that said, "If Necessity is the mother of invention, Devastation is surely the father." Nothing is more true as it was the devastation of losing my father and the necessity of my children and the people that I came in contact with that caused this book to be birthed.

It may surprise some of my family and friends to know that this book that I've written isn't *necessarily* a Christian book nor is it a religious book. It is, however, a book based on a set of principles that I have come to learn and now know to be true. Its very foundation is built upon a wisdom that is so solid and unshakable that each chapter must start with it or it would be without a base, foundation or cornerstone. I pray with everything within me that the words between these pages prove to be as much of a help to you as they have been to me, my family and will be for my own children, grandchildren, great grandchildren..............

Your friend and Brother,

C. Joseph Simpson

~1~

Come Let Us Reason Together

Romans 12:2

And be not conformed to this world: but be ye transformed by the renewing of your mind.

Many people, married and single, look at a marriage certificate as, *just a piece of paper.* Well, I hate to agree with so many people on a negative statement in the beginning of such a positive book. The truth of the matter is that a marriage certificate *is* no more than a piece of paper *if that's all you consider it to be.* Why do so many people look at a marriage certificate as just a piece of paper? Could it be that we don't understand the nature of the union? Since we don't understand that, we actually depreciate the value of it and therefore fail to use the same tenacity in picking a mate as we do in picking out a car or house. Another point to consider is why once we make the final payment on the house or car, the first and last thing we make sure the finance company gives us is the title to the car or the deed to the house? When we get the deed or title, why do we put it in the safest possible place we can find? After all, *it's just a piece of paper, right?* Wrong! That piece of paper represents so much more.

That *piece of paper*, the title or deed, is symbolic of your tenacity to do thorough research and your ability to make a sound decision, which represents maturity. It displays your ability to use drive and determination to see something from start to finish, which is a representation of accomplishment. That *piece of paper is* also emblematic of your ability to maintain someone else's property (because the bank owns the house or car until you're finished paying for it) which represents selflessness. Most of all, we keep it in a safe place because that same *piece of paper* represents ownership. Ownership isn't a bad thing if you look at it in its correct perspective. Ownership means it is yours and nothing or no one can take it from you. It also means that you will do anything and everything within your power to prevent anyone from trying to take it from you.

MAN! If we had that same sense of ownership with our marriage (not ownership of the person we're married to but of the marriage itself) we would have far less divorces than we do now. This leads us to one of the major issues that will kill any marriage. Some people simply will not take ownership. We've moved entirely too far into the 'I'm not doing this alone' business. Think of two people going into business with one another. Both persons have invested a substantial amount of time and money but the business is still beginning to fail. What do you think would happen? They would at least make an attempt to find a way to salvage their business. What if one of the partners wasn't showing any real concern? The other partner would do whatever was necessary to protect his or her own interest and investment in the business. That's taking ownership. What I find so disturbing is that as people read this, they can relate to a greater degree of ownership of the car, the house or the business but not the marriage, especially when the former three are temporary and the latter is (or can be) a lifetime. Marriage has the potential to be so much more than what we make it out to be if we would just invest the same time and effort we invest in other things such as possessions. As a financial wizard might say, we would receive a greater return for our investment.

Marriage is a beautiful institution that has been entrusted to man by one that is all knowing and all wise. Marriage has been given as a gift to us and we have been given as a gift to one another. In his infinite wisdom, the Creator made mankind into social beings. The term social being means that we are interdependent of one another because of our social needs. You can be a brain surgeon but if your basic plumbing goes bad, you will be dependent upon the plumber to assist you. The plumber will be dependent upon the accountant to do his taxes and the accountant will be dependent upon the mechanic if he has any issues with his car. Think of how much *more* help a loving spouse actually is to the dependence of his or her partner. That is truly a gift. This very dependence we have of one to another predetermines that we will have no choice but to interact with one another. This fulfills one of man's divine duties, which is to be fruitful and multiply. This basic duty and command of being fruitful and multiplying carries one of the greatest misconceptions and because of this misconception it is one of the greatest hindrances known to man. This grave and weighty misinterpretation will be dealt with in Chapter 3 while dealing with the purpose of marriage.

It is no secret that the divorce rate in America is alarmingly high and has been on a constant and steady climb for years. This means that something in the preparation of those entering matrimony is either lacking or missing altogether. They are being set up for failure before they even make it to the altar, if they get that far. Something is seriously wrong in the grooming of our young men and women in their preparation for life and marriage. Scripture says that you can tell a tree by the fruit it bears. If a tree is yielding bad fruit, it's not the fruit that needs to be examined. You need to examine the tree! Every older generation that has something to say about the younger generation, no matter how young the older generation is, needs to check themselves and analyze the example of what is being left behind.

The clinical definition of insanity is "Doing the exact same thing over and over again and expecting a different result." I posed a question to my son one day. I said, "If I were to walk over to the light switch, turn it on and look at the television to see if it came on, what would you think about me?" He said, "I would figure that you didn't know what the light switch was for." I said, "Now what if you told me what it was for and I still went back to that *same* light switch and turned it on and off again while still looking for that *same* television to come on? What would you think about me then?" My son in his infinite wisdom looked me directly in my eyes with a stern yet puzzled look and said, "I'd think you were crazy" and he was emphatically correct in his youthful deduction.

So many of us in our senseless and careless concern for our lives continue to flick the *same* light switch on and off and expect that television to come on. We take that same failed approach with our future, our health, our children, our finances, our relationships and so many other aspects of our life. We continue to flick that light switch we call *habit*, look at that television we call *life*, and expect it to come on with a perfect picture in some *spooky* mysterious way and we've deceived ourselves because it's not going to happen.

In order for us to get a different result from what we do in life, we must rethink and use a different approach. My father used to say with his deep Southwest Louisiana accent, "If you always do what you always did, you'll always get what you always got." We have to understand that we are a conglomerate of habits. Everything we do in life is a developed habit regardless of if the habit formed is good or bad. I heard someone say, "If you don't consciously make good habits, you'll subconsciously make bad ones." So many of us have developed bad habits concerning relationships and marriage that they now have become the norm and are now being manifested in our high divorce rate. This *Marriage Manual and Handbook* is an honest attempt in the assisting of breaking old bad habits and in creating more productive habits concerning our marriage. First, we have to acknowledge that we may have *possibly* developed some bad habits and have made some bad decisions concerning our relationships. Next, we have to get to the *why* of the matter. We have to find out why we developed the bad habits in the first place. Once we determine why we created these habits, then the third step is to learn how to break them. The fourth step is to implement what we have learned by creating new, productive habits and then just to continue to improve.

How can a bad habit hinder a person's life? If a building is built on a poor foundation, it may stand for a little while but time and pressure will surely bring it to its ruin. The Leaning Tower of Pisa began construction in 1173. The tower began to sink that year because the soil was unstable and the foundation was too shallow. Because of wars and lack of finances, construction had to be halted but the tower still stood with a slight lean for a hundred years. After that time, construction began again to erect the tower. Because of time and pressure added, the tower continued to lean adding a millimeter to its lean each year. The tower now leans 14 ½ feet out of line. As they continued to erect the building, they tried to compensate in the structure itself by making the upper floors one side taller than the other. The building now has a curve in it and the problem still wasn't fixed. What was the original problem? The original problem for the tower is the same problem for many of our marriages, relationships and even we as participants in these relationships. We may not want to admit it but the truth of the matter is *we have poor foundations* which establish our bad habits.

Before we begin to feel bad about ourselves, there is some good news. The good news is that it is not our fault nor is it too late. We are just like the regular workers that worked on the tower. We weren't taught to do calculations, risk estimates and land surveys. We were just told to, "Nail that over there and hope it stays up." Come, let us reason together; we have to admit that in all our doing that something can't be right if the failure rate for marriages is over 50%. That's a hit or miss probability. Do we really want to base giving someone that we haven't known our whole lives all of our love, all of our trust and all of our heart on a 50/50 chance? That's the possibility of investing too much time, pain and emotion for nothing.

How about we try something different? Instead of just adding on to an already defective building and having it curve and lean on us (it's going to fall anyway), how about we just examine our foundation? This time we can build one that will not only withstand the trials of time but will also withstand the added pressures that are sure to come with life. It all starts with the very next chapter, Know Thyself. That chapter is the key to rebuilding your foundation. It will help you understand who you *think* you are and who you *really* are. That is the only way you'll be able to pinpoint why you have created the habits you have created, why you have done what you have done and why you continue to do what you do. The third chapter, Understanding the Purpose of Marriage, is equally as important as the second. How in the name of anything holy can you want something when you don't even know its purpose? Not what you think its purpose is but the actual purpose of it. I can think all day that the purpose of a screwdriver is to hammer nails into the wall. I can use it for that purpose and it may work for a little while but eventually I'll get tired and frustrated with it. I won't get tired because I'm not trying. I'll get tired because I'm not using it for what it was actually designed for. The fourth chapter is to assist in making the mental calculations of choosing a mate. It also lays out the foundation and basic process of going from dating to courting and from courting to matrimony. If chapter 4 isn't understood, it could very well be or mark the beginning of the end. Chapter 5 is written on the subject we bring up the most when talking about getting married, love. Love is truly the glue that holds marriages and any other relationship together but sadly it is one of the least understood subjects in the entire book. The basic foundation of even understanding love has been lost in romance novels, movies, television shows and even the possible twisted versions of what we have witnessed while growing up. Chapter 6 is about the male/female wants, needs and desires and chapter 7 assists with achieving those desires by serving as the section that defines the roles and responsibilities of a husband and wife. Without those two chapters there is no way possible of knowing how to fulfill our mate's basic needs or desires therefore leaving them empty and void. Chapter 8, the longest yet most needed chapter, is on communications. This chapter assists in recognizing communication breakdowns, communication repair, defining proper communications and the rebuilding of communication lines. Chapter 9 is all geared toward understanding the cause of many of our divorces, adultery. It shows how adultery will never solve your marital problems but shows how people, sometime innocently, continue to fall into that same trap of an affair. It even explains the shocker of how it is easier for a woman to fall into the entrapment of an affair than it is for a man. Chapter 10, The Conclusion of the Matter, will bring everything together and cement the entire process from start to finish.

I pray that the use of this Marriage Manual & Handbook proves to be fruitful and a great help. I pray that it helps us to identify some of our bad habits we have collected concerning our relationships. Many of the habits that we have picked up along the way are either from our own cognizance or from people we have met while embarking upon this journey we call life. Most of these people probably didn't mean any harm and were probably misinformed themselves. I hope that we are able to determine why we have adopted these habits and then break them when they are identified. I finally hope and pray that this body of work will assist us in implementing the new habits we have found and continue to improve on them on a daily basis. In the essence of the matter, in order to have different results we must first accept the fact that what we have been doing may not have been the most beneficial to our desired end. However, in order for us to arrive to our desired end, we must transform our thinking. I humbly submit to you that the only way to transform your thinking is by renewing your mind.

*And be not conformed to this world: but **be ye transformed by the renewing of your mind. Romans 12:2***

Why do I think I have adopted my bad habits concerning marriage and relationships?

Let's go to the next chapter and see if we are correct......

~2~

Know Thyself

1 Thessalonians 5:23
And the very God of peace sanctify you wholly; and I pray God your whole spirit and soul and body be preserved blameless unto the coming of our Lord Jesus Christ

Before we begin, let's just close our eyes and imagine something for a minute. Let's imagine that you open your eyes and you wake up in a hospital bed. You feel a slight lump on your head and notice strange people around you. One man, that you assume is a doctor, asks you do you know where you are. You struggle to answer, "I guess I'm in a hospital." "Good", he says but then asks you if you recognize any of the people in the room. You feel a little uneasy because you don't recognize them but then fear sets in because you realize you are unable to know who you are. That would be a frightening thing. I know that I exist but I don't even know who I am.

It would be an insane assumption to think that you understood yourself when you don't even know yourself. Two of humanity's greatest questions are, "Who am I and why am I here?" It is the 'Why am I here' (or what is my purpose) part that has baffled mankind sense the beginning of time. Yet, we'll never get a true glimpse of the answer until we answer the 'Who am I' question first. The sad state of the process however, is that we have the cart before the horse. Too often we accept the limited knowledge of what we know about ourselves as truth. The information we have might be a fact but not necessarily Truth. For example, the fact of the matter is that I am C. Joseph Simpson and I was born in Southwest Louisiana. This is a fact but if some documents were found that stated that I was actually adopted, then that fact is no longer truth. A fact is a fact as long as nothing supersedes or proves it to be otherwise but truth is truth no matter what. So yes, we may have the facts of who we are but do we really know the truth of who we are.

Why is self-knowledge so important to understanding purpose and why is purpose such an intricate detail of our foundation? The answer is simple. A screwdriver will never be used to the fullest potential of its purpose until it is realized that it *is* a screwdriver and you will never be used to your fullest potential until you realize who you are. Once you realize who you are, you can then maximize your full potential. Once you are able to maximize your full potential you will be able to define not only your purpose but also your role and responsibility in the greater purpose of marriage, which is why you picked up this book in the first place.

Now let's get back to our scenario of you waking up in a hospital bed and suffering from amnesia. You are told these people are your family and that you would be going home soon with them. When it's time to go, you put on your right sock and right shoe and then your left sock and left shoe. The older gentleman that the doctor told you was your father looked at you and chuckled, "Some things never change." You don't know why you did it but something that was ingrained in you deeper than the thoughts you think manifested itself. This strange thing is called a habit. Habits are real and powerful. Good habits will be the key to your successes while bad habits can be the catalyst of your downfall. Bad habits can be frustrating once you realize that the habits you developed over the years are bad and counterproductive to your success. They are also usually a little harder to break than most people think. A wise man once said that the easiest thing to make is the hardest thing to break, a habit. Habits can be a great thing if you use them to your advantage. Good habits can be the thing that put you over the top in your profession, education, finances, relationships and any other area in your life. Just as they are there to build you up, your habits can and will be the very things that will tear you down.

Your habits are so deeply ingrained in you that you barely have control over them or yourself unless you make a strong, conscious effort to deviate from them. How many times have you been driving home, started to daydream and in the middle of your trip you realized that you were driving on something like autopilot? How did you blank out for minutes and arrive to where you are now? You were driving on instinct or habit but what do habits have to do with knowing yourself and why or how is this going to fix your relationships? It's all intertwined.

If I should know myself, then who am I? If you believe that you are a child of the most high God, then you are off to a good start. The problem with this is that most people usually stop right there. We say that we are children of God but what does that actually mean? The scripture says that 'God is a Spirit' and if that is true, then I must be a spirit also. Why must we be what He is? We must be because scripture says that we are created in His image and after His likeness. We were also created with the purpose of having dominion and operating in the earth or this new physical world.

*And God said, Let us make man in our **image**, after our **likeness**: and let them have **dominion** over the fish of the sea, and over the fowl of the air, and over the cattle, and **over all the earth**, and over every creeping thing that creepeth upon the earth.* **Gen 1:26**

If we are created in His image and His likeness then we must be just like Him or *reflect* what He is. It's just like the picture of you on your wall is a reflection of you or an image of you burned on paper. You are a reflection of Him burned into a manifested reality.

You may say, "Ok, I understand that I'm created in God's image and that my habits will affect me positively or negatively. What I do not understand is how this will affect my marriage". To fully grasp this, we have to extract all truth about who we are. Once we understand who we are, then we can determine why we make the habits we make. This will in turn determine why we do what we do and make the decisions we make, before, during and after marriage.

The first thing we have to understand is that we *are* created in the image and likeness of God. We have to conclude that and understand it without the shadow of a doubt. Next, if we believe that we are created in His image and after His likeness then we have to settle that we are just like Him. At this junction the most crucial thing for us to understand is that *God is a Spirit* (John 4:24). Now if we believe that and we believe that we are created in His image and after His likeness then again we have to understand that if God is a Spirit then we are spiritual beings as well. It's quite interesting that even though we may not say or even believe that we are spirits, somewhere in the back of our minds we already know this and are to a certain extent aware of it.

Have you ever gone to the funeral of someone and looked at the person in the casket? This could be someone that you probably knew all of your life and you said to yourself, while you looked at them in the casket, *he's gone* or *she's gone*? How can you conclude that after you see the deceased person in the casket, the same person that you saw all of your life, that they are now gone? It's because somewhere in the back of your mind, you already know that the *real* person isn't lying there in the casket or the *real* us isn't this heap of flesh that we walk around in. We know that the *real* us (the spirit) is in us (the body) somewhere.

God says through the Prophet Jeremiah that before we were formed in our mother's womb, He knew us (Jeremiah 1:5). A child is formed in the womb of its mother only after conception. If this is true, then he knew me before I was formed. Then it's also safe to conclude, that He knew me before I was conceived. The only way He can know me before I am conceived is if I exist before I am conceived. I humbly submit to you, that the only way for me to exist before I was formed was for my spirit to exist before the conception of my body. We could go so much deeper into this but this is not what this book is about.

Now we determined that we are a spirit and now understand that the spirit is the real us. The spirit is the one that existed so much longer than before we were conceived. After we were conceived, a body was formed. This body that was formed is the thing (and I mean *thing* because it is not the real person) that we thought we were all of our lives here on Earth. This thing that we call body is no more than a suit that we (the spirit) put on.

Let's look at it this way. If someone said that they were building a new civilization on the planet Mars and the trip was all expense paid, many people would jump at the offer. In order to survive when they got there, they would have to wear this special suit so they could be sustained. The suit will cover them from head to foot but they will never have to take it off because the inside of the suit is self maintained and self cleaned. If you gain weight, the suit will stretch with you. If a baby wears the suit, it will grow with them all the way through adulthood. All the owner of the suit has to do is wash and clean the outside of the suit and take it in every year to a specialist for a checkup. The checkup is done at a facility where specialists insure that the inside of the suit isn't being damaged or is deteriorating. What do you think will eventually happen? People will begin to identify more with the suit than they would with the real them. Every time they looked in the mirror to wipe the suit down, they would see the suit and not themselves. Every time they talked to another person, they would see a suit and not the real person inside. Eventually they would come to a point where they would begin to believe that the real 'them' is the suit and not the person inside of the suit. That would be easy to do because when a child is born in the 'facility', it would be placed in the suit by the specialists before the mother has a chance to hold it. So from birth to death, the person is in the suit. Throughout their whole lives, the person is in the suit. When the suit can no longer maintain itself, the person inside is shipped back to earth. The suit is placed inside of a box and all of the family and friends come to view the suit one last time. People even have a 'good bye' ceremony as they come to view the suit. People will come from far and near to look in the box, *see* the suit, cry and say to themselves, *he's gone* or *she's gone*.

Now since we have some clarity from the above scenario, remember the *real* us are spirits but we are made to operate in the earth or this physical world. In order for us to operate in this physical world, we (spirits) would now need a physical body or suit. This suit or physical body ensures that we will be sustained during our sojourn here on this physical planet called Earth. Herein lies the problem. In order for us to be sustained, one of the body's main functions is to maintain itself. That's why when you cut yourself the body automatically starts to heal itself. Again, this shows that the body's primary function is to simply take care of itself. The body is a highly functioning, technically sound machine and is as self sufficient as any other highly functioning, technically sound machine. When the body is starting to become depleted of nourishment, it will send a 'low fuel level' signal to the brain and call for food or drink. When the body has been operating too long and energy is starting to diminish, it will begin to shut certain departments down and will even recharge itself by resting. You may say, "What's so profound about that? That's natural." That's true. It is natural but remember we are spirits, not natural or of nature. Our bodies are natural but *we* are not. Natural or nature means *of the external world in its entirety* but we aren't of the *external* world, we are the *internal* spirit.

The problem is that we've been thinking all of this time that we were our bodies, so we operated in the capacity of our bodies. Remember one of the body's main functions is to sustain or take care of itself. Not only is the body's main function to take care of itself but if unchecked, it will *only* take care of itself. This is what we call selfish. Unchecked, the body will only do for self and it has to be that way because the body was designed to replenish itself and operate in this physical world. Remember, the spirit is of God and like God. Left to itself the spirit would only want to do the things of the Spirit, *constantly* and with no deviation. There's nothing wrong with that. That's what the spirit was designed for, to do the things of God because it is of God. Remember the spirit lives in the body and if the spirit had its way, the body would probably starve and be broken down from lack, because the body wouldn't be allowed to replenish itself.

Between the spirit and the body, there are two extremes that are at constant odds with each other; the extremes of selfishness and the extremes of selflessness. If I constantly do what the body wants (selfishness), I would physically survive but I would be no different than the animals. I would be driven by my appetite and give in to every animalistic lust that my body craved (Gal 5:19-21). I would be headed on a quick path to self destruction. If lead entirely by the spirit (selflessness) and not give concern to the body, we would have peace with ourselves and our fellow man but our bodies would go lacking and would eventually decay and die.

The way it is now for most of us is that we are led by our bodies or flesh and let our spirits scream muffled warnings in the form of, what we commonly call our conscience. Sometimes we listen to this conscience and sometimes we don't. This means that sometimes we suffer adversity in our lives and sometimes we don't. Remember being led by the appetite only brings us to a path of self destruction and no good can come as a result of that. So what is the happy medium? The happy medium is to be led by the spirit *and* be concerned with the body. This will lead us to a fruit filled life (Gal 5:22) and still maintain the needs of the body and not so much as the wants. It's when we give in to all of the wants of the flesh that we resort to our lower self which is driven by appetite. Now the million dollar question is what is the happy medium and how do we get there?

And the very God of peace sanctify you wholly; and I pray God your whole spirit and soul and body be preserved blameless unto the coming of our Lord Jesus Christ. **1 Thessalonians 5:23**

Notice, the scripture refers to our spirit, soul and body. We've determined the difference between the spirit and body but what is the channel between the spirit and body? Most of my life I thought the soul and spirit were one in the same but you can see that distinctions are made among these three entities. We know that the spirit is the real us and will continually be righteous in spite of all. We know that the body is this house of flesh that we live in and will give in to every whim of appetite no matter how low and detestable but what about the soul? The soul is where flesh *meets* spirit. It is that area where flesh comes in to try and dictate to spirit and the area that spirit attempts to come in and lead flesh. The soul is the actual battleground of flesh and spirit. They put on their full armor and meet there and battle on a daily basis. They even battle many times a day. Every decision is a battle. Before a word is spoken there is a battle and before actions take place, there was a battle. We are fully aware of this battleground and even have a name for it. However we don't call it a battleground but that's what it is. Some call it the soul. Some even call it the conscience or heart but to reference this entity in laymen terms; we call it THE MIND. This is where the spirit and flesh duke it out on a daily and continual basis.

It is in the mind that the flesh will attempt to manipulate you into doing something in accordance with the appetite or something that you know is wrong. Yet, it is in that same mind that your spirit (you may even call it your conscience) will convict you to do what is right even when you want to do something wrong. Have you ever done something wrong and knew that it was wrong yet did it anyway? You have to answer yes because we all have done something of that nature. If you *knew* that it was wrong, why did you do it anyway? The reason is the same for any situation and for any person. We rationalized doing wrong in the darkness of our mind and allowed our flesh to win a certain battle. It's on that battleground, the mind or soul, that wrong decisions are rationalized and validated before they are implemented. It's in the soul or mind that flesh will gain a foothold in your life and bring you down or the real you, your spirit, will gain a foothold and bring you up.

This is where many of our issues come from within our relationships and marriages. We've allowed our suits or flesh to dictate our actions. If I am married and another person of the opposite sex is as attractive (attractive in how they look, what they may say or how they carry themselves) as my spouse if not more attractive, it's **natural** that my suit will gravitate to that other person. My *suit* is designed to gratify itself in every possible situation. My suit is created that way but my spirit tells me that the *real* me is not. Remember, my suit is selfish by nature and it has to be that way. It is designed to maintain itself and will give in to itself in every way, situation and circumstance. If my spouse makes a comment that could be taken a few ways, the suit automatically goes into a defense mode and launches another verbal attack because it *perceives* that it was threatened. Even if I make a genuine mistake, the suit will anticipate a *perceived* threat and begin to tell lies to defend itself from an attack that may never happen. Since my suit is designed to maintain and gratify itself on a continual basis, it will even attempt to manipulate others in different ways so that some type of gratification will come to it.

Every time you cater to your flesh, guess what you are creating, a habit. Every time you cater to your spirit, guess what you are creating, another habit. These habits we are creating are molding and shaping our character. They are defining who we are, how we will be in relationships and how we will react to certain situations. The greatest thing that needs to be understood is that every time you react using a habit (whether it's good or bad), you reinforce it. Every time you decide *not* to give in to a certain habit, you weaken it.

I once heard it go like this. An old man was speaking to his grandson and he said, "Little one, there are two wolves fighting inside of you. One wolf is good and the other is evil." The little boy became concerned and asked his grandfather, "Which one will win grandfather?" The grandfather looked at him and said, "Whichever one you feed." The wolves can represent our habits. If we feed our good habits, those will become stronger. If we feed our bad habits however, they will begin to take over our lives. What is our ultimate goal for success in our lives, feed our good habits and starve our bad habits.

The good news is that a good habit is nothing more than the opposite of a bad habit. One challenge is going to be identifying the bad habits because to us, everything we do is normal. Even though our actions in our relationships may not be working, to us they are still normal. Now, changing from a bad habit to a good habit is not quantum physics. Once the bad habit is identified, just do the opposite. It's as simple as that. The hard part won't be to just do the opposite. The hard part will be to win the new battle in the mind that will actually *permit* you to do the opposite. I've come to realize that most bad habits people develop in relationships are really just defense mechanisms. Some past traumatic experience have left them with a PTSD (Post Traumatic Stress Disorder). It's like a person that has been shot before but survived. They now literally feel naked if they don't have their bullet proof vest on. The vest is now their *automatic* defense mechanism. That's what may be the hard part; getting it in your mind that you will be alright if you take your armor (bad habits) off. It's because of this piece right here that I used the quote by Kalil Gibran in the very front of this book. If you haven't read it, please take the time to go back and read it.

A relationship can be scary enough and marriage can be a horror when thinking about exposing yourself. It's in a true relationship or marriage when two people are able to stand spiritually, mentally and emotionally naked in front of one another. Why, because, it's the person that I reveal the most to that can hurt me the most. They will know all of my fears, personal scars, wounds and weaknesses. If I reveal all of that to them, they will be able to use all of that against me and potentially cause more pain than the original wounds. However, if I keep my armor on, they will not be able to see my wounds. Therefore, they will not be able to use my wounds nor my words to hurt me again but neither will they be able to get to my wounds to tend and dress. If I don't take my armor off, they will be unable to assist me in my healing. Your spouse should be your 'help meet' and that statement will be qualified and appreciated so much more in the next chapter. If you didn't read the quote at the beginning of the book, please go back and read it. This one sentence comprising of four lines is one of the most powerful lessons you will ever learn of marriage and relationships.

The battles of flesh and spirit takes place on a battlefield called the *mind*. If you don't understand anything else, understand that. Wars are waged in the soul or mind countless times a day. The soul is the area where thoughts are pondered upon. It's where feelings and emotions are rationalized. It's deep inside you where you know what you know because of how you think, feel or believe. The soul is where decisions are made based on whichever, spirit or flesh, wins the battle in a particular war. When these decisions are made and then implemented, you are in the beginning stages of forming a habit. These habits will either cultivate you and your relationship or destroy you both. You are ultimately responsible to decide which habits stay and which habits go. You are the captain of your ship and the guide of your own journey. You will either choose daily to cultivate good habits to take you closer to the destiny you desire or to continue cultivating your bad habits which will continue sabotaging your relationships and keeping you alone and unproductive.

Do I truly understand that I am a spirit that always wants to do right yet have a body that always wants to feed its own appetite?

More importantly, do I truly understand that the battle ground of the two is in my mind and the winner of each battle is shaping all of my habits, both good and bad, on a daily and continual basis?

~3~

Understanding the Purpose of Marriage

Genesis 2:18

And the LORD God said, It is not good that the man should be alone; I will make him an help meet for him

Myles Munroe once said, "If you don't understand the purpose of a thing, *abuse is inevitable.*" Although any type of abuse is dangerous, it's the subtle abuses that are a little harder to put a finger on and therefore harder to repair. In my opinion, the word abuse can come from two words; abnormal and use. Any time you abnormally use something, you are actually abusing what you are using.

Question; is it possible to make grilled cheese sandwiches in a toaster? Yes, it is but that's not what the toaster was designed for nor is it the purpose of the toaster. It's an abnormal use of the toaster. After a while, all that melted cheese will start to take its toll on the toaster and the toaster will eventually begin to break down. In the beginning you might not even notice the declining productivity of the toaster. You may not notice it for a while but a breakdown is happening. The alarming thing is that all this time you thought everything was alright because you were getting grilled cheese sandwiches.

That is why fully understanding the purpose of marriage is so vital to the perseverance of the institution. If a couple doesn't understand the purpose of marriage, abuse in that marriage is inevitable and it may not always be blatant abuses but it may be abuses that are subtle and not so easy to detect. It may be those subtle abuses that creep in like weeds. You know how it is. One day you have a beautiful garden. It's so beautiful you don't worry about maintenance. You're so captivated by its beauty you hardly even notice the little sprigs pushing its way through the ground until one day you notice it's overrun by weeds and it seemed to happen overnight.

This is how it is in many marriages. We get so captivated with the idea of being in love and being married, we don't define its purpose nor do we calculate the maintenance required. Understanding the purpose is vital because it will assist in characterizing our roles and our roles will define our responsibilities in maintaining our spouse or pulling maintenance on our marriage. So what is the purpose of marriage?

And the LORD God said, It is not good that the man should be alone; **I will make him an help meet** *for him.* **Gen: 2:18**

The purpose of marriage is to have someone assist you and even more so for you to assist them in the fulfilling of their own God given purpose. The *help meet* will be expounded upon in a few paragraphs. Let's first discover what a marriage is. Marriage in itself is a covenant and when two nations go into covenant with one another, each nation promise to perform a certain duty for the other. If Nation A's strength is agriculture and Nation B's strength is military prowess, they may go into covenant with one another. Nation A agrees to supply food to Nation B and Nation B will provide defense for Nation A. What if the nation with military expertise begins to fail in its part of the covenant? The agricultural nation may begin to send less food to its defenders. Once Nation B gets less food, they will defend even less, which will cause Nation A to send an even smaller amount and so on. This causes a break in covenant or as we commonly call it…divorce.

Most marriages start off with good intentions. Most people that get married want to do what's right in the marriage but then a covenant is broken because one or neither party even knew that they were in a covenant. They just knew that they were in love (which **is** a good start) and wanted to be together but didn't really understand why. It's the "why" that gives marriage its solid foundation, its purpose and assist us in defining our roles.

Let's look back at our nations in covenant. Nation A supplied the food and Nation B supplied the defense. If Nation B did its duty to the best of its ability and gave Nation A the best defense possible, most likely Nation A would make sure Nation B was well fed. When you give the nation you are in covenant with your best, more than likely the other nation will give you their best in return. It's when one party starts to feel like they are being taken for granted that the covenant begins to break down.

Let's look even deeper into the purpose of marriage. When the scripture is read:

*And the LORD God said, It is not good that the man should be alone; I will make him **an help meet** for him.* **Gen: 2:18,**

It is usually interpreted as the woman was created to help the man and this is true to a certain degree but this is base knowledge of that scripture. Let's go deeper and glean all of the hidden nuggets from this passage. Remember from the first chapter that we are spirits; we live in a body and we possess a soul. Why do I need this physical body if I'm really a spirit? When God created this physical world, he put us in physical bodies to have dominion in this physical world and rule in his place.

*And God said, Let **us** make man in our image, after our likeness: and let **them** have **dominion** over the fish of the sea, and over the fowl of the air, and over the cattle, and **over all the earth**, and over every creeping thing that creepeth upon the earth.* **Gen 1:26**

Because God created this physical world He gave us (spiritual beings) physical bodies to use in this physical world much like that space suit we talked about in the previous chapter. What does this have to do with the first scripture of this chapter and why doesn't this mean that the woman was created to help the man? To fully understand the first scripture **Gen: 2:18** you have to fully understand the second scripture **Gen 1:26**.

In the second scripture, **Gen 1:26,** God said let us make man and let *them* have dominion. We often hear people explain the "us" in that sentence but we rarely notice the "them." If God only created one man thus far who was the "them" he was talking about? If the passage is read carefully, the words *him, man, them* and *Adam* are all synonymous and actually mean mankind. This is explained in the next verse.

*So God created **man** in his own image, in the image of God created he **him**; male and female created he **them**. **Gen 1:27***

God says concerning the creation of man that he created *him* (mankind) in his own image. Then the scripture says that male and female created he *them*. So Adam is not only the first man but also the first made people or the beginning of mankind. This is proven even further in Genesis chapter 5.

*This is the book of the generations of **Adam**. In the day that God created **man,** in the likeness of God made he **him**; Male and female created he **them**; and blessed **them**, and called **their** name **Adam**, in the day when **they** were created. **Gen 5:1-2***

Why is it pertinent for us to understand these passages? Because Genesis 2:18 answers a few questions about purpose. This scripture encompasses the Law of First Mention. Anytime something is first mentioned in the bible, this is pretty much a certainty of how it is supposed to be.

*And the LORD God said, It is not good that the **man** should be alone; I will make **him** an help meet for **him**. **Gen:2:18***

God said that it wasn't good for man (mankind) to be alone. He didn't say it was impossible but it wasn't good rather. Because of this, God said that He would make 'him' an help meet for 'him'. So we are also created to be a help meet for ONE ANOTHER. Now that we have a better understanding we realize that it's not just for the woman to help the man but also for the man to help the woman and he refers to the spouse, be it male or female, as the help meet.

Now this is a different use of language; help meet. He didn't say partner, mate or even help m-e-a-t. He said help m-e-e-t. We understand what help is. Help means to assist in an endeavor but what is 'meet' and why is it used? It is interesting to know that this translation for meet only appears twice in the bible and both times it used in the same instance, as in concerning a spouse. This English word meet is translated from the Hebrew word *ezer*, which derives from the root word *azar*. *Azar* is Hebrew for help but not only help but to literally run and help. So when God created a help meet, he created a helper that would literally run to and help the one he was supposed to help. So my main purpose for being a spouse is not only to help my spouse but also to run and help my spouse; it's to give the advantage and not take the advantage, as my Pastor says. If no one else in the world will run and help my spouse in a time of need, I should be breaking my neck to get out of the starting gate before anyone else.

What am I to help my spouse with may now be the question? The first thing God told man after he created him was to be fruitful and multiply.

And God blessed them, and God said unto them, **Be fruitful, and multiply***, and replenish the earth, and subdue it: and have dominion over the fish of the sea, and over the fowl of the air, and over every living thing that moveth upon the earth.* **Gen 1:28**

Most of the time we read this and think God is talking about having children. That's true to a certain extent but that is the base level of that scripture. We've proven that if we can't do anything else, we can do that. However, what is the deeper meaning of that scripture? Fruit are the manifestations of a transformed life *(Gal 5:22)*. Remember the real you is a spirit, therefore the fruit we must be full of is spiritual. One of my teachers taught me that fruit must be cultivated. Weeds can grow wild and independently but effort has to be put in the cultivation of fruit. The passage didn't say have fruit. It said be fruitful or full of fruit. That means

I must actively and purposefully cultivate every area of my life if I'm to be fruitful or full of fruit.

Now what is the 'multiply' in the command "Be fruitful and multiply?" Another one of my teachers taught me that having children is the base level of multiplication for this scripture also. He said that multiplication has a formula. The formula is:

a Multiplier   X   a Multiplicand   =   Product

If this is a true formula for multiplication then our purpose is given. Let's apply the formula to ourselves now. It would be I (the multiplier) x the multiplicand (which is this universe and all that God placed in it and in me) = product or *Productivity*. My true purpose is to be productive in all that I do. This purpose goes in direct correlation to what comes next after man is told to be fruitful and multiply. God says next:

And God blessed them, and God said unto them, Be fruitful, and multiply, **and replenish the earth, and subdue it: and have dominion over the fish of the sea, and over the fowl of the air, and over every living thing that moveth upon the earth. Gen1:28**

As one that God placed in the earth with dominion, I am to rule and govern. I am to have authority in the earth and be God's ambassador and rule as he would. Before man is given dominion in the earth or told to subdue the earth, he is also told to replenish the earth. What does replenish mean? It means to refill, to restock or to make better.

If I could sum up my whole command from He who created me I would have my whole purpose. First of all I am to cultivate myself and transform my life into my true spiritual self. I am to be fruitful in every area of my life, productive in all that I put my hands to do, efficient in making this world a better place and a representative of Him who created me. That is our own God given purpose. Since we have our individual God given purpose, we now also have the purpose of a spouse and therefore the purpose of marriage. As a spouse, we are supposed to first, *run* and help our spouses to meet their individual purpose. This *run* means that we should forsake all others if given a choice of helping more than one person. No one should come before my spouse in any area of my life. Secondly, we are to use our gifts and talents in assisting our mates in the pursuit of their individual purpose. We should assist them in becoming the most balanced and productive persons that they can be. Third and most importantly, we should also be willing and trusting enough to allow our mates to speak into our lives by giving us good and wholesome instruction or counsel. Therefore, the purpose of marriage is to give assistance as well as get assistance in the fulfillment of our own God given directives.

Before we end this chapter it must be said that if you are attempting to fulfill what God has placed in you to do and *are* on the path of where He has told you to go, then you are ready for a spouse to help you meet your goals and responsibility. However, if you are neither on the job placed before you nor on the path that you are directed to go, then, what do you need a spouse for, to help you meet nothing, go nowhere, and do nothing? In this case, you don't *need* a spouse. You only want one for some base need and in the end that need will surely be for something selfish. Someone who needs a help meet is someone who not only needs help meeting a purpose, a duty and a goal but also someone who doesn't mind helping someone else meet their own purpose, duties and goals.

Question: Do I truly understand my God given purpose, the purpose of a spouse and most importantly the purpose of marriage?

Let me explain.

~4~

Take Them to Court

Genesis 4:1
And Adam knew Eve his wife; and she conceived, and bare Cain, and said, I have gotten a man from the LORD.

I remember when my father told me how he met my mother. He said they moved from the country to the city when he was a teenager. He and some friends went to the movies and he saw this beautiful girl that took his breath away, as he described. He just had to meet her. He nervously approached her and her friends and started a conversation. During the conversation he found out that she had recently moved back to the city as well. Was this coincidence or fate? I assume my father thought it was fate because his later actions proved his thoughts. He asked the young lady if he could walk her and her friends home. She allowed him to walk her home only if he would buy her an ice cream cone. He agreed which proved to me that he thought this chance meeting was more than coincidence.

You see my father grew up very poor in rural Southwest Louisiana during the late 1930's and 1940's. My grandfather died early leaving my grandmother and her 10 children alone to fend for themselves. My father had to quit school in the 3rd grade to help out the rest of the family to tend the land until they moved to the city. What we may consider to be a mere ice cream cone was an investment to my father. He couldn't afford to be frivolous with money. Every dime had to count and it did, including the money for the ice cream cone so many years ago.

My father bought my mother the ice cream cone, she allowed him to walk her home and they talked all the way to her house. He asked if he could see her again, she said yes and he would stop by to talk under the supervision of my mother's sisters or one of her brothers. Then they would talk for hours, which seemed to go by like minutes. They talked about their past, their present and the possibilities of the future. Whether they knew it or not, these two people employed a very strong premarital principle which just isn't used anymore. This principle, in my opinion, could raise the success rate of marriages dramatically if applied. The name of this principle is rarely used anymore and the activity of this principle is almost archaic. This is the simple yet effective principle of *courting*.

When speaking of courting one may make the statement that people don't do that anymore or that's old fashioned. They may also make the statement that they actually thought they *were* courting. Whether you thought it was old fashioned or whether you thought that you were actually doing it is of no effect if you don't understand what it is. Let's look at the base word of Courting, which is Court.

Court-
-A large open section of a building, often with a glass roof or skylight or
-A formal meeting or reception presided over by a sovereign.

The word court has several different meanings but we'll expound on the two definitions above. The first definition says a large open section of a building, often with a glass roof or skylight. Notice the open section of the building has no walls, no closets and even the roof, if it has one, has a glass ceiling or skylight. This means that it is *totally open*. There is nothing hidden, nothing obscuring your vision and all is disclosed in the court. Court is also defined as a *formal* meeting. When you hear the word court the words informal or casual never enter your mind. A court is also a place where two parties come together to display evidence or facts before one another to make a certain determination. There is nothing informal or casual about that setting either. In recent times there has been a misconception or misunderstanding of courting. People now assume courting is the same as dating and this is the furthest from the truth. If this is your understanding, then you are skipping an entire portion of the process that has been specifically designed for a purpose.

Before we go on we have to agree that process and procedure are extremely important. The sad thing is that everyone won't agree with process. They say, "I found someone that I find attractive and that I like." They also think "We'll just let nature take its course." Remember from Chapter 2 we're not of nature. We don't do things the natural way. That's what animals do. They find a mate that is suitable for their needs at that time; they mate and then go about their business. That sounds all too familiar to the way a lot of us are doing it now. We find someone that suits our needs, we mate and then we go about our business or get married if the mating lasts long enough.

Let's discuss process for a minute. If you wanted to bake and eat some bread you have to follow a process. You first gather the ingredients, next you mix your ingredients, then you bake it in an oven and lastly you get the bread out of the oven and enjoy. All too often many of us *skip* the baking process or we'll put the dough in the oven but take it out before it's ready. Then we wonder why we're not happy when we're married. It's because we're eating dough. A process was skipped or the process didn't fully mature.

Before we attempt to tackle courting, let's first understand the relationship process. Skipping this process is where many of the first mistakes are made. The proper procedure is a basic three steps which are to go from Strangers to Acquaintance, then from Acquaintance to Friend, then from Friend to Life Long Friend or Companion. As the old saying goes, it is better to marry a friend.

Strangers => Acquaintance

Acquaintance => Friend

Friend => Life Long Friend or Companion

Now let's use Webster to define each part of the process.

1. Stranger- *One who is **unknown** or unacquainted; as, the gentleman is a stranger to me; hence, one not admitted to communication, fellowship, or acquaintance*

2. Acquaintance- *personal knowledge of **information** about someone or something; a relationship less intimate than friendship; a person with whom you are acquainted*

3. Friend - *a person you know well and regard with affection and **trust**; ally: an associate who provides assistance; a supporter*

Let's get back to our steps. A stranger is someone that you know absolutely nothing about. You may never talk to them if opportunity doesn't present itself. In the bread baking stage, this is where you simply want bread. You have nothing tangible. You just want some bread and that person is simply a stranger. Now if opportunity presents itself or you just decide to interact briefly with that person, that person will now become an acquaintance. You may learn their name, where they're from, where they work and so on. You're basically gathering information like you gather ingredients to bake the bread. Now, since you're acquainted with that person you have the option of interacting more and more with them if you choose. This is where you're checking the consistency and texture of the dough after all ingredients have been gathered and mixed together. You want to make sure it's even worth going into the oven or going into the friend stage. When baking bread, you may have found out that you don't have any yeast or there is too much water. In your acquaintance stage, you may have found out that your acquaintance is missing a quality you would enjoy in a friend or may have too much of a quality that you wouldn't want in a friend.

Placing the dough in the oven stage, like the friend stage, is crucial and an expensive time of development. Let's say your oven can only use wood for heat and you only have so much wood and none to spare. You wouldn't waste that wood on dough that you know wouldn't bake good bread. You wouldn't waste all of your time and the little bit of wood that you do have on dough that you know you're going to throw away. You would be a little more selective of the dough you bake and you should be equally as selective of the acquaintances you make into friends. You could possibly waste a whole lot of time and effort on people who don't deserve to be your friend. This is why this stage is expensive.

Let's go back to the stranger stage for a second. If you saw a stranger that was rude, obnoxious and just had a bad personality, would you go out of your way to get acquainted with that person? No, you would feel that person wasn't even worth getting acquainted with. You would stop them in their tracks. You wouldn't let them get to know you nor would you want to get to know them. Well, once you're acquainted with someone and you're not sure if you like what you see, you should slow down from allowing them into your holy of holies or the inner circle of your friendship. You also need to know that there are different levels of friendship. As an acquaintance you gather information about the person you're dealing with and you're also presenting information about yourself to them. During the *acquaintance* stage your acquaintance should be proving himself trustworthy of being a friend. Even as a friend, they should continually prove themselves to be admitted to your inner circle.

Even Jesus practiced this principle. In Mathew 26:36-39, Jesus left the multitudes and went with His twelve disciples to Gethsemane to pray. Once at Gethsemane, He left the majority of His disciples and took only three a little farther. Once He got a little farther, He dropped those three off and went even farther to be alone with God (His Father, His friend, the one He had full trust in). In this instance the multitudes represent strangers and acquaintances; for what is an acquaintance except a stranger whose name you know. The disciples represent friends and the different levels of friendship. Peter and the two sons of Zebedee represent the inner circle of friendship and God is a true representation of the one He let into His Holy of Holies. God is the one He had the ultimate trust in and could honestly call His companion.

Notice the closer He got to His inner circle the smaller the group got. It's just like a pyramid. All of the strangers and acquaintances are at the base. It is broad and wide. As you go up it begins to get narrow. To be honest, the movement from acquaintance to friends and the different levels of friends (the middle of the pyramid) may even get a little blurry at times because this is the proving stage. In the proving stage there is a constant shifting and shuffling. People are constantly proving and disproving themselves. We may not make a full note of it but a constant mental calculation is going on unbeknownst to our conscious mental state of being of whose company we keep (*Proverbs 12:26*). The danger arises when we override the decisions of these subconscious and sometime conscious computations. We'll have an example of this later in this chapter.

So we decided we wanted bread to eat. We gathered all of our ingredients. We did a proper mixing and decided that the dough has the right ingredients and consistency. Now we can eat and enjoy, right? No! You don't enjoy eating dough! You have to bake it first, using two primary mechanics, heat and time. When we talk about heat we're not talking about sexual heat. That simply put is *lust*. Scientifically speaking, heat is the transference of energy. This is where dating ends and Courting begins. Dating a friend is fine. Dating is where you're checking the consistency of the dough. You're just going on dates enjoying your friend's company. This is why they call it *dating* but when you want to see if the person you're dating would make a good companion or spouse, you transition from dating to courting and courting takes *energy*. Remember heat is energy transferred.

If there is too much heat, the bread will burn and if there is not enough heat, the dough will not bake. Moving from dating to courting is like turning on the heat in the oven. There must be a state of *transference* that is understood by all parties involved. Note the transition from kneading the dough to placing it in a hot oven. There is a distinct transition point where all parties are fully aware of the changeover. The baker is aware when he feels the heat and the bread is definitely aware. It's at this changeover that Courting actually begins. This is where we move from dating (enjoying each other's company) to Courting (investing energy and time).

Courting is where time is invested. It is where, as we stated before, evidence is laid out for all to see and all to investigate. It perplexes me that people will invest more energy in investigating which car or which house to buy. They may only keep the car or house for 5 to 10 years but will invest relatively no time in deciding on the spouse they are supposed to stay with for the rest of their lives. Sometimes they'll even get married on a whim because they don't want to be by themselves or they don't want the person they're dating to be with anyone else either. Both reasons are extremely selfish and the City of Matrimony has no place for a selfish citizen.

When the Courting phase starts, all preliminary bases should have been covered by this time. The person I'm dating is no longer a stranger. I've acquired all of the information that I need of this person so we are past being acquaintances. This person has proven to me and I've proven to them over and over again that we can be trusted in words and deed. When they have fallen short, they were quick to repent and honest in the approach of the reconciliation of our relationship. Therefore, I can now consider them a true friend. We've also been spending a lot of time together and I really enjoy their company. STOP! Now is *not* the time to get married. If both parties decide that the relationship can go to the next level, it is now the time for a shift. It's time for you to transition from dating to courting and determine if this person is marriage material.

Before we make the official transition into courtship we must remember the two previous chapters. First of all, I must know myself. Secondly, I must know the purpose of marriage. If I don't know myself, then I won't know what my wants, needs and desires are or what makes me happy other than surface happiness. How then can I expect someone else to assist in my happiness or assist me in going where I should go? That would be impossible if I didn't know what made me happy or where I should be going myself? Also, if I don't understand the purposes of marriage, I'll abuse it. I'll be looking for someone to complete me, someone to edify me, someone to build me up and someone to fill a void that I myself have no idea what a person needs to bring to fill that emptiness. I won't understand that I'm in a covenant where my primary goal is to edify my spouse and understand that in return my spouse will do the same for me. I won't understand that in a covenant I am responsible to perform a certain duty to my spouse and in retrospect my spouse will in turn perform a duty to me. When we both understand this, then we should be able to enter into a healthy, beneficial, meaningful covenant.

When one person is unsure of what marriage or a covenant is, it leaves the duty and responsibility on the shoulders of the other person. This causes the burden bearer to feel as if they are being taken for granted and often times overwhelmed in the relationship. For this reason all questions should be answered during the courtship, so that there will be no misunderstandings. In dating, all we expect is a good time and all too often we go from dating to marriage expecting a good time and that good time may never manifest itself because there is a missing link, the courting process. This process is an extremely important part of marriage. Getting married without courting is like attempting to build a house with no blue prints. You're going to just go with your feelings. Now we may say that it's insane to build a house on feeling and with no blueprint but it's just as insane to attempt to build a marriage without courting. Nothing has been planned, nothing has been measured, nothing has been laid out, and nothing has been taken into account. As a result, we're going to just *feel* our way to building this house or this marriage. No! We must prepare or do the prep work before one nail is nailed in. I understand that this may be a hard pill to swallow and a lot of work involved but in the carpentry world there is a saying, "Measure twice but cut once." This means that you should take the time to measure at least twice just to be sure of your measurements before you cut any piece of material once. Once the piece is cut, it's done and permanent, be it right or wrong. How does this fit into our equation? Dating is measuring once. Courting is measuring twice. If you do this you should only cut (get married) once. If you only measure once (date) you may have to cut two or three times. You may even have to start with a whole new piece of wood if you cut too much off.

Now all of this is good and practical information but what does the word of God say about Courting. Our base scripture for this chapter says,

And Adam knew Eve his wife; *and she conceived, and bare Cain, and said,* **I have gotten a man from the LORD**. *Gen 4:1*

The scripture says that Adam knew his wife Eve. Adam didn't just lay with her or go into her as other parts of the bible speak about conception. The passage says he knew her. Knowing someone denotes a deep, intimate knowledge of something. We can also ascertain from this passage that Eve didn't become his wife *fully* until he knew her. The passage says Adam *knew* Eve his wife and then the translator used a semicolon. If you don't understand what a semicolon is used for, the whole point may be missed. A semicolon is for a stronger pause than a comma but not the stop of a period. It is also used to bring in two separate ideas into one common idea or two *separate* sentences into one sentence while remaining grammatically correct.

Let's dissect this passage and see what we can extract. The word knew is the past tense of the word know but what is the definition of the word know? Know means:

1. To **perceive** directly; to grasp in the mind with clarity or certainty. 2. To **regard as true** beyond doubt. 3. To **have a practical understanding** of, as through experience; 4.To have fixed in the mind: 5. To **DISCERN the character** or nature of.

In order for Adam to know Eve, he had to come to perceive or understand her for himself. He had to regard what he perceived about her to be true beyond any doubts in his mind. He also had to have a practical understanding and be able to discern the character of her nature. The definition says, *to discern the character or **nature** of* but we have to understand the character *of* our nature. We have to be as sure as we can *possibly* be of how our future spouse will operate when he or she operates spiritually or naturally (or fleshly). If what I said didn't make sense, it is imperative that you go back and read or reread Chapter 2 "Know Thyself". You have to grasp Chapter 2 for it is the base knowledge of understanding the sum total of why we do what we do. We have to have a good knowledge base of how our future spouse will exemplify their character in spirit and in flesh.

Once Adam actually came to the point where he *knew* Eve, then and only then did she fully become his wife and they were able to come together and conceive. Hold on Brother Simpson. Eve was called Adam's wife many times before the book says he knew her. Yes. I understand that but for you to fully understand it you have to understand Jewish tradition. Jewish tradition declares a relationship goes through a time of betrothal which is equivalent to our engagement period. Both engage and betroth means to promise and prepare to marry. This means that both parties declare exclusivity, promise to marry each other and begin to make preparations for their new life together. The difference between betrothal and engagement is the legality of it. In an engagement the exclusivity is understood but in a betrothal it is legally bound. The only way to get out of a betrothal is to have a legal divorce. In a betrothal the two parties are considered married in a sense but can't physically come together until after the betrothal period.

This is why there was such a controversy around the birth of Jesus. Mary was betrothed to Joseph. They were pledged to be married but neither could be physically intimate with another person nor could they physically come together themselves (not legally). This is why Joseph contemplated quietly putting her away or in other words, divorcing her when it was found out that she was pregnant with Jesus. The betrothal period was not to be taken lightly in those days and neither should the engagement period of our day be taken lightly.

Let's get back to our scripture. Remember it said,

> **And Adam knew Eve his wife**; *and she conceived, and bare Cain, and said,* **I have gotten a man from the LORD. Gen 4:1**

Now we've dealt with the first part of the sentence and determined that Adam knew Eve, in every sense of the word, before they officially consummated the marriage. Let's now deal with what happens after the semicolon or the second sentence in that sentence. Eve conceives, bares Cain and says that she has received a man from the Lord. Most people seem to think that Eve was talking about receiving the child but this will be the only reference in the bible of speaking of a child and calling him a man. The closest reference of calling a child a man is calling the child a 'man child'. This is because Eve may not have been talking about Cain. She may have been talking about Adam. Adam is the man that she received from God. Adam was the man that God created and predestined for Eve to be with. He was the man that God breathed wisdom into, the man that God took her out of and the man that God brought her back to and be betrothed to. This is another interesting point in itself. God took Eve out of Adam and then brought her to Adam.

And the rib, which the LORD God had taken from man, made he a woman, **and brought her unto the man. Gen 2:22**

This is beautiful symbolism that we usually just glaze over. The father of Adam is God. Yes, that is understood but God is also the Father of Eve. Most times we just glaze right over that part. God or Eve's daddy brought her to the man denoting his approval of a spouse for his daughter. This is why the daughter should heed the council of her father or that male father figure in her life before betrothal or engagement is established. The man that has been responsible for taking care of the young lady either physically, spiritually or mentally is also responsible for making sure the next man will take care of her from then on. Proverbs says,

*; But in the **multitude** of counselors there is **safety**. **Proverbs 11:14***

After God brought Eve to Adam, they went through their time of betrothal. We don't know exactly how long that was but we do know it was at least two chapters. They were betrothed in Genesis Chapter 2 and they came together in Genesis Chapter 4. What happened in Chapter 3 that Eve would say in Chapter 4 that she received a man from God? If you look in Chapter 3, this is where the fall of mankind takes place. Eve was beguiled by Satan and yielded herself to her flesh. In her confusion she caused her husband to stumble also and be severely chastised by God. This is almost too quick of a synopsis of this story but it does leave room for another book. In all that confusion, weakness and betrayal, Adam stayed with Eve. When they were cast out of the garden, Adam could have abandoned Eve leaving her vulnerable and fending for herself. When she saw that Adam had seen her at a very low state and was able to look past her shortcomings *(and she was able to look past his, remember Adam knew what God had commanded in the beginning but he still blamed Eve when God showed up and Eve knew the command also but she still offered fruit to her husband, so they were both wrong)* and stay with her so she could say, "I have gotten a *man* from God." "I received a man in every sense of the word; I have received a man that will look past my faults; one that will not judge me and will still provide for me; one that will make me feel secure and assist me in being the woman that God has ordained me to be. I have gotten a man from God". Only after Eve was able to come to know Adam through chapter 3 and Adam would come to know Eve that they could *fully* come together and conceive.

Now this is what happens when people go through a courtship before they get married and come together. What happens when there is little or no courtship? Our best example is the strongest man in the bible, Samson. If you study the life of Samson, you will see that he was a sucker for a pretty face. As a matter of fact the first words out of Samson's mouth were, "I have seen a woman. Get her to be my wife." Some scholars would argue that Samson getting this Philistine woman was God's plan to get back at the Philistines. Yes, it was God's plan to get back at the Philistines but not for Samson to murder 30 men because of his new wife's trickery. Much could have been avoided if Samson was betrothed or courted in the manner he should have according to his tradition.

Next, Samson was almost murdered because he was involved with another woman he hardly knew and the 3rd woman who brought the fatal blow to Samson was Delilah. Delilah was the woman that Samson fell in love with but also barely knew. She sold Samson out for money and brought about his downfall. God had such great plans for the great judge Samson but he wasted it on his loins. Yes, he killed a few thousand Philistine rulers but his people were still confined by their enemies when he died.

This is what happens when we don't court our future mates. We have to understand that getting married is a serious process. We can't just skip parts of the process because we feel it takes too long or we have a good feeling. We have to respect process because it has been put in place for our benefit. Skipping a step in the marriage process is like putting four tires on your car with one bolt on each tire because it *feels* like it will take too long to put the rest of the bolts on. You may say, "I can't afford to waste time putting all those bolts on the car. It will take too long." Brother/Sister, you can't afford *not* to put all the bolts on or you may wind up like so many other cars on the road to matrimony; an accident just waiting to happen.

Do I truly understand the Purpose and Process of Courting?

Let Me Explain.

~5~

What's Love got to do With It?

1 John 4:8
He who does not love does not know God, for God is love.

It's safe to say that when you ask someone why are they getting married, why did they get married or why do they stay married, love will come up 90% if the time. I've learned that people are liable to say anything for the other 10%. So let's deal with Love since this is the reason the majority of the people use to get married or stay married. Don't get me wrong. Love is a good reason to get married and also to stay married. However, with the divorce rate being so high and people saying they are marrying for Love; one would have to ask, are we really marrying for Love or do we really understand what Love is?

This chapter is entitled, 'What's Love got to do With It' because Love has a lot to do with it. Before we determine what love has to do with it, we have to determine what Love is. Webster makes an attempt to define love as:

Love - *a strong affection; an attraction based on sexual desires; an affection and tenderness; a warm attachment or an object of attachment, devotion or admiration; brotherly concern for others or unselfish, loyal, benevolent concern for the good of another.*

Mr. Webster almost got it right at the end. Before we determine what love really is, let's determine what love is not. First of all, love is not an emotion! Every time someone begins to describe Love, words of emotion come up; the way I feel about a person, the feelings I get when I'm around the person or the feelings I get when I think about the person. If Love is an emotion, then let's look at some other emotions and see if love can pass the emotion's litmus test. An emotion is a state of mind like happiness, anger, sadness, eagerness and even pain to name a few. If these qualify as emotions then we can see that all emotions come and go. We are never always happy, angry or sad nor are we in pain continually. Emotions are forever changing. They come and they go depending on the situation or circumstance that we are in.

If this is the case then we can see why people fall in and out of love at the drop of a hat or as fast as they fall in and out of bed. They may be confusing Love with something else, like an emotion. This is why we can be confused and claim to be in love with two people at the same time. It's because we have lowered the standard of love to an emotion and we have to agree that love is supposed to be something that lasts. If love is supposed to last and emotions are ever fleeing then love can't fit that category.

Before we go deeper, let's continue with our litmus test of love being an emotion. Our second test shows that emotions can be a noun, such as, "the *anger* of the people" and the most it can be is an adverb but never a verb. As an adverb we may say, "He *angrily* left home" describing how he left but never a verb. You can't say, "I angry you" or "I happy you." An emotion can be a noun or an adverb but never a verb. Love on the other hand can either be a noun, an adverb and most importantly, a verb. As a noun we can say, "The love of the people". As an adverb we may say, "He lovingly called her name", describing how he called her. As a verb we can use our favorite, "I Love you", like any other verb denoting action.

The third and final test is the effects of Love and emotions. Simply put, emotions nine times out of ten, affects you directly. Love however, nine times out of ten, directly affects others. This will become clearer as we go on in the chapter.

This being said we have to agree that Love doesn't pass the litmus test of being an emotion. Since it doesn't pass the test of being an emotion then it can't be an emotion. What we've been doing is associating the emotions and the affects that accompany Love with Love. We've been letting how we *feel* about someone determine if we Love them or not. This is the biggest misunderstanding of Love and it stems from a childhood behavior. I can hear you thinking right at this very second, "I'm not a child." Well, you may not be a child but let's look and see if your understanding of Love is childlike.

As a child, a ten-year-old boy in elementary school looks at a pretty ten-year-old girl. She looks into his eyes and smiles at him. This causes him to get butterflies in his stomach. He says, "I *must* be in love." He watches her for a few days and finally gets the nerve to talk to her. He introduces himself shyly and she extends her hand to shake his. BOOM! Fireworks shoot off when their hands touch. Now, not only does he have butterflies but now his heart beats faster, and he starts to sweat. "I *know*

57

I'm in love now", he says. Now every time he *thinks* about her he gets butterflies. He's still in love right? As far as he's concerned he is. Now what happens when he begins to get use to her and those butterflies start to subside? Sooner or later he'll lose those butterflies altogether and guess what? He loses interest and he's not in love anymore. He never was! This is nothing more than human infatuation and a child's perception of Love. Though we may call it love childishly, many adults share the same view of Love and fall in and out of love as often as we fall in and out of bed. It's still that same childish infatuation except the *boom* may be a little bigger and the fireworks a little more intense.

As the child gets older the sparks from the fireworks will progress from hand touching to kissing and from kissing to more sensual, stimulating types of touch. I don't think that I have to go into any more detail than I already have but the outcome will still be the same. He will eventually stop having those feelings and conclude that he is no longer in love. You cannot base if you're in Love by how you feel. If your relationship is built on some base level gratification or feeling, then what's going to happen when what's gratifying you doesn't *quite* gratify you the way it use to? It's going to happen all over again. You will conclude that you are no longer in love and it's been happening to you ever since you were in middle school. Many still define love as we did in middle school. It's not your fault when you've never been taught about Love and just left to yourself to figure it out. Oftentimes all you know is what you know and what you know is all you know. The sad part is that a lot of times *what you know is all you want to know.* This is when you become stagnant and mentally dead and in need of some type of resurrection. In my humblest opinion, I submit to you that maturity will assist in your mental resurrection.

Side Note:

*Maturity is when you are able to take someone else's opinion and experiences into consideration. You don't have to do what they said or do what they did but at least take it into consideration. This shows that you are mature enough to look at your situation from all angles and sides even if it contradicts your own thoughts, belief and opinions. You can now make the best **informed** decision and you understand that you can't be totally informed unless you have all possible information.*

Let's get back to our discovery. We have discovered that Love is not an emotion. We have discovered that most of the time love affects others outside of ourselves and we have also discovered that Love can be, most importantly, a verb unlike emotions. So what is Love? Love, according to C. Joseph Simpson is "A Perfect Expression of Itself." You may ask, what is a perfect expression of itself? Let's look at it.

Perfect- *being **complete** of its kind and without defect or blemish; without qualification; Lacking nothing essential to the whole; **Pure; undiluted**; unmixed;*

Expression- *The act of expressing, **conveying, or representing** in words, art, music, or movement; **a manifestation**; the outward manifestation of a mood or a disposition;*

If we were to use these two definitions as our guide, then Love would be a complete, pure, undiluted representation or manifestation of itself. With that being said, Love is a "Perfect, proof or evidence of itself. Ok, that's good but what does that have to do with Love being a verb? Let's go to our scripture for this chapter, *1John 4:8* which says, *God is love.* Now this is extremely profound. It didn't say that God showed love or acted with love. It says that God *is* Love. Why is this so profound? You see, you can put a suit on a monkey and the monkey may act human or show human qualities but the monkey is still a monkey. Acting a certain way or showing certain qualities doesn't nullify who or what you actually are but the scripture says that God *is* Love. Well, if God is Love then

59

Love must also be God. Now if we truly understand that God is Love and Love is God, then now we have to be careful. We can no longer throw that word around to be used to manipulate others for some selfish and base reason.

Now we have to get to why *is* God Love? We have to go to one of the best known scriptures in the world, John 3:16. It says, *"For God so loved the world that he gave his only begotten son…"* It says that God loved the world so much that He *gave*! There is a manifested proof of God's Love. It didn't say that God loved the world so much that He *said*, "I Love You"; it said that He 'gave'. The Love of God promoted an active verb *gave*, and then there was a manifestation, "His only begotten son." One of the largest problems in the world today is that too many of us are using the word love as a noun or an adverb. As a noun or an adverb it may sound good and even look good but there is no active force which will bring about some manifestation of what I say. This is how a man can say to a woman, "I Love you" and she can enjoy what she heard and yet still feel unloved, empty and even cheap in some instances. It's because there is no manifested action after his statement that will bring about a visible proof of his Love.

Now that we understand that real Love requires action and brings about manifestations or results, let's go a *little* deeper. Galatians 5:22, 23 says,

*22But the fruit of the Spirit **is** love, joy, peace, longsuffering, gentleness, goodness, faith, 23Meekness, temperance: against such there is no law.* **Gal5:22&23**

This scripture says that the fruit of the Spirit *is* love, joy, peace, longsuffering, gentleness, goodness, faith, meekness and temperance. Take notice of the word 'is' in that passage. The word 'is' is a passive

60

verb that denotes third person singularity. Now what does that mean? This means that if I'm talking *to* someone about *one* other person, that is third person (singular). In this particular case I would have to use the verb 'is', like, "She is hungry." If I'm talking to someone about *some other* people (plural), I couldn't say, "They *is* hungry." I would have to say, "They *are* hungry." This would denote plurality yet still speaking in third person.

The Apostle Paul in his letter to the Galatians didn't make a grammatical error when he penned this particular passage. Yes he used a verb intended for singularity but his subject was also singular. What was his subject? Look at it closely. His subject was *fruit* and not *fruits*. He said, 'the *fruit* of the Spirit *is*' not 'the *fruits* of the Spirit *are*'. If he said that 'the fruit of the Spirit is', then what are all of these fruits he brought up such as love, joy, peace, longsuffering, gentleness, goodness, faith, meekness and temperance. Before we answer that question, let me ask you another question. Do you know what an Amplified Bible is? An Amplified Bible is a bible that will amplify, define or exhaust the meaning of a word so that the reader won't miss the intent of the author or the true meaning of a word. It is amplified for the benefit of the reader.

Now let's get back to our original question. What are all of these fruits if he was talking about one fruit? Let's read it again.

*22**But the fruit of the Spirit is love** (STOP), joy, peace, longsuffering, gentleness, goodness, faith, 23Meekness, temperance: against such there is no law.**Gal5:22&23***

When you get to the word Love, you can stop reading because the scripture is actually finished but Paul amplified and defined the actual fruit, Love, for us. So we wouldn't miss the meaning of the word, he exhausted its definition. So when we read it we can say, "But the Fruit of the Spirit is Love." After he said that, one could ask, "Well, what is Love Paul?" So Love can't be misconstrued to have some base meaning, he defined it for us. He said that Love is *joy, peace, longsuffering, gentleness, goodness, faith, meekness and temperance.* Then he ended the sentence by saying, "Against such there is no law." This means that when you are operating by the fruit of the Spirit which is Love, then you don't need some law to mandate your actions. Love will do it for you. You don't need some outside entity to assist in guiding and regulating your behavior. If you are truly operating in the spirit, then Love will regulate your every deed, thought and motive.

Let's bring this back into perspective now. Remember we said that most of the time Love will affect others. Well, how do you think that you will be able to affect or love others until you first Love yourself? I think that needs to be said again. *You will never be able to love others until you first love yourself!* Can you give someone apples if you don't first have apples? It's the same with Love. You can't give someone something you don't first have yourself. If you tried, you would only be giving them some low emotion and now we know that emotions do not last. However, if you were operating in the spirit and you gave them the *fruit* of that Spirit, which is Love, then you would *ensure* that whoever you claimed to love (and that should be whoever you come in contact with if you are truly operating in the Spirit – especially your spouse) would have *joy* and *peace* in every area of their life. You would *suffer long* with that person when dealing with their faults and shortcomings. You would be *gentle* and *good* to them. You would have *faith* in them and be *faithful* to them. You would be *meek* or walk in humility with them. You would also display *temperance*, which is nothing more than self-control, when dealing with them. If you truly Love someone, in the truest sense of the word, you will ensure that you display all of Love's attributes to the one you claim to love. We should take our example of love from God and His Christ. Remember, God so loved the world that He *gave* and Christ so loved the world that He *sacrificed*. Even when He was being betrayed, He prayed for those that betrayed Him *because He loved them*. He didn't stop loving them when the butterflies went away or when they stopped praising Him. He said, "I love you and then with corresponding actions, He proved it."

Do I truly understand what love is?

Let me explain.

~6~

Wants Needs and Desires

Gen29:14-18

After Jacob had stayed with him for a whole month, 15 Laban said to him, "Just because you are a relative of mine, should you work for me for nothing? Tell me what your wages should be." 16 Now Laban had two daughters; the name of the older was Leah, and the name of the younger was Rachel. 17 Leah had weak eyes, but Rachel was lovely in form, and beautiful. 18 Jacob was in love with Rachel and said, "I'll work for you seven years in return for your younger daughter Rachel."

Now we've reached the core and pendulum of this book and of all doomed or failed marriages. The number one reason that marriages fail is that people do not get to the root cause of their problems. So many times we put a band aid on a gunshot wound and wonder why the patient died. Let's look at it this way. I'm driving my car on the highway and my oil light comes on. I say to myself, "I'll check it down the road." A few miles go by and the oil light is now accompanied by a loud, annoying buzzing sound. I still don't have time for maintenance so I stop the car, open the hood and cut the wire that is going to my oil light indicator switch. I get back in the car, *Ahhhhhhhhh, peace, quite and tranquility. Now I have no annoying, flashing, red light and no irritating buzzing sound.* Did I fix the problem? No! I fixed a symptom and purposely ignored the warning signs. However, the problem still exists and is getting worse by the minute. Now however, I have nothing to alert me of the severity of the problem. The next alert will be the sound of my engine locking up or the sound of someone knocking on my door serving me divorce papers, all because I chose to ignore the warning signs.

Let's look at another scenario. You just purchased a new shirt. You pull out all of the stickpins and put the shirt on. You realize its cold outside so you layer yourself with other clothes. You put on your pants, sweater, jacket, overcoat, gloves and a hat. You get ready to walk out until you feel this sharp pain in your side. The most important question you can ask yourself at this time is, *why*. Why am I feeling this pain? You take off your gloves, hat and overcoat but you still feel the sharp pain. Why am I still feeling pain? You take off your sweater and you'll still feel pain. Again you ask yourself, "Why am I still feeling this pain?" It's not until you take off your new shirt and examine it that you realize you missed one of the pins. Taking all of the layers of clothes off and then taking the shirt off is like getting to the root of the problem. What if you took off all of the layers but never examined the shirt? Yes, you would have discovered the root of the problem. You would then realize that the shirt was the problem all along and then simply put it back on. Guess what. Your problem is back and you're still in pain because even though you identified the problem, you failed to correct the situation.

These two scenarios capture both sides of the coin. The first scenario, with the oil light, represents the spouse that may be causing the issues and missing or ignoring the warning signs that the disgusted spouse may be giving. The second scenario, with the stickpin, represents the spouse that may be getting fed up with something in the relationship but doesn't go deeper to find the root cause of the problem or attempt to do anything about it until it is too late.

Neither scenario is healthy but the situation is all too familiar on both sides. You will have a spouse that knows their partner is unhappy. They may not know exactly why but the tell tale signs are there. The unhappiness may manifest itself in nagging, being argumentative or the slamming of objects around the house. All of these are quite loud and can't be missed. There are some silent tell tale signs also such as the upkeep of the house, the upkeep of their personal appearance or just silence itself.

No matter what the signals and signs are, they can't go on ignored. The spouse, whether wittingly or unwittingly may have already sown the seeds of discontent in the heart of their partner. The stems of frustration will soon push through the ground of matrimony. Once the stems of frustrations reach full maturity, it's *almost* impossible to prevent the fruit of divorce. Once the fruit shows up we already know what's inside of the fruit, the seed multiplied. What was our original seed, discontentment? Now, it's going to come back multiplied because we allowed a seed to be sown and we let it go unchecked.

Galatians 6:7 (CEV)

7You cannot fool God, so don't make a fool of yourself! You will harvest what you plant.

The root cause of most divorces is a void in what I call the 'Core Intrigue System'. Some would read this and say, "No, our reason for getting divorced was because of money or infidelity, lack of commitment, lack of communication" or an assortment of other reasons. That may be true but these are all symptoms of the true illness. The true illness is the emptiness of the Core Intrigue System. Anytime there is a void in this system, something will take on the task of filling it. What usually fills the emptiness are the very symptoms that we blame our divorces on. Just what is the Core Intrigue System? First, to understand the system, you must first define the words of its makeup. The *core* is the base or central part of a unit. *Intrigue* is to arouse the interest or curiosity of something. Taking this into context and you get the Core Intrigue System or the central part of what arouses our interests.

There are three parts of our Core Intrigue System. They are our 'Wants', our 'Needs' and our 'Desires'. Most people only understand these three separate entities at the surface and are unaware of their extremely close relationship. This may come as a shock but some people even think that they are all one in the same; synonyms if you will. In all honesty, their meanings are so close that they may get confused in definition and intent. Because of these misunderstandings, we will not be able to go any further until they are each defined and understood. Until we characterize each and put them in their proper perspective, the reader may continue being confused and lost in translation. So let's first define each.

1. **Need** - Something **necessary or required**; a physical or psychological **requirement** for the well being of an organism.

2. **Want** - To **feel the need** for something; to have a strong desire; to feel something is necessary.

3. **Desire** - A **mixture** of Needs and Wants;

Wants Needs and Desires

Let's look at an example of what has been defined; something such as a car. Let's say I *need* a car to get back and forth to work. This need is pertinent to my well being and the well being of my family therefore, a necessity. My *wants* however, are to look sharp and smooth while I ride in my car; so now I *want* an Escalade. I know I need a car but I really want to look sharp while I'm driving. An Escalade is slightly out of my price range but I know I can afford an Escalade if I make sacrifices. Now, my wants start to *feel* like needs and my needs become secondary to my wants. All of these mental calculations of wants and needs have now become my *desires* or my Core Intrigue System. Once we have our desires, our minds are made up to what we will pursue *regardless* of whether our desires or good for us or not. We will always go after our desires and that is the reality of our makeup. The danger appears when our desires are made up of more of our wants than our needs. Remember our desires are a mixture of our wants and our needs. It's also important to understand at this point that our needs are pertinent to survival and our wants are by nature selfish.

How does trouble come into play? Let's go back to our example. I need a car for the well being of my family. I want an Escalade to look sharp and smooth while I ride. An Escalade is slightly out of my price range but I feel that I can afford it if I make some sacrifices, so the Escalade has now become my desire. By nature I will follow after my desire (and not my good sense) and 99.9% of the time I will be led away by my desires *(James 1:14)*. What I didn't calculate was how great I would have to sacrifice to afford the Escalade. Now my finances run low and it's starting to cost me more to keep the Escalade than I'm making. My desires have now become a burden as they often do.

How do these wants, needs and desires affect relationships? Let's go to our foundational scripture for this chapter, Gen 29:14-18. We find Jacob, the son of Isaac and grandson of Abraham, on the run. Why he's on the run is a totally different story but he winds up at his uncle's house and meets two young women. I submit to you that these two young women can be symbolisms of Jacob's wants and needs and will ultimately become his desires.

Let's look at the situation. Jacob flees to his uncle Laban's house. Upon his arrival, Jacob meets and falls in love with one of Laban's daughters (Yes his cousin ~ I didn't write the story). The names of Laban's daughters are Leah and Rachel. Leah is the older daughter. By custom and tradition, she should be getting married first. She is not the most attractive but she is the most fertile and the one that should be married first. Rachel, on the other hand, is the younger of the two daughters. Rachel is more attractive than her older sister Leah but is not as fertile. Let's look at the backdrop of this scenario. At this time in the Middle East, a man's wealth was dependent on his livestock. If he came from humble beginnings, he couldn't afford to hire workers. He would have to have many sons to assist him with his livestock if he wanted a chance at becoming wealthy. The more sons he had, the bigger his stock could be. Let's get back to our story. According to tradition, Leah should be getting married first but Jacob's desire was to marry the younger, more attractive sister, Rachel.

Now, let's look at Jacob's core intrigue system. Jacob *needs* a wife that will bear him many sons because at this stage of his life he can't afford to hire help. However, he *wants* a wife that has a beautiful face, figure and anything else that will please his eyes. Jacob makes a deal with his uncle Laban. He tells Laban that he will work for him for seven years for the hand of his daughter Rachel. Laban agrees and Jacob works seven years, as required, only to have Laban live up to half of his agreement. Laban did give Jacob his daughter but not the daughter he wanted. Jacob's wants were so great that he not only worked seven years for Leah, the daughter he did not want; afterwards, he also agreed to work an additional seven years for the hand of Rachel, the daughter he originally wanted. A lot went downhill from there. Let's just look at the downward spiral on the surface level. Jacob wasted 14 nonproductive years of his life to fulfill a want. If he would have just fulfilled his needs first or let his needs outweigh his wants, he could have attained his wants also at a much lower cost. Laban said that it was better to give his daughter to Jacob than some stranger, so he was Laban's choice anyway. All Jacob had to do was marry Leah, his needs, first. He wouldn't have had to work for Rachel, his wants. After the bridal week, Laban would have given Jacob Rachel also with no labor required. When Laban saw how stupid Jacob was for Rachel (wants), he figured he could get another 7 years of free labor from him, which he did. What did Laban have to lose? He already married off the oldest girl. Jacob's desires for his wants were so great that he made an unnecessary deal to work 14 years for the same girl. Anytime your wants outweigh your needs, unnecessary stress is soon to follow.

This chapter, next to the communications chapter, will probably be the longest chapter in this book because understanding wants, needs and desires can be detrimental if not understood. Even though understanding wants, needs and desires are imperative to understand for the survival of a marriage; they are either totally disregarded or not placed in a weightier category as they should be. If people asked themselves this next question when choosing a mate; can this person fulfill my needs (Not my wants but my needs)? At the very least, 50% of the divorces could be avoided. The important thing to remember is that we all have desires and our desires are made up of our wants and our needs. Also remember that discontentment will eventually strike when our wants overshadow our needs. Within our desires, our needs should outweigh our wants or at the very minimum, they should be equal. Am I insinuating that a couple can't have a relationship if a person's wants outweigh his or her needs when choosing a mate? That is the furthest from the truth. This is where you come in as an individual. Only *you* know what *you* will put up with and what you will do without for what length of time. What I am saying is that many of us will purchase that Escalade knowing that all we *need* is that *dependable* Accord. We may have to eat beans and weenies for dinner but we can put up with that for the sake of the Escalade. We'll get that good looking, fine or wealthy mate to take care of our *wants* and then wonder why our *needs* aren't being met or why we have stress in our marriage. It's because we've allowed our wants to overshadow our needs.

I think we now have a good understanding of wants, needs and desires. I also think that we now recognize how crucial it is to get a firm grasp on the meaning of these words and how they play out in our lives. Since we have a good understanding, let's look at the specifics as they relate to the male and female relationship. There is no way possible to look at the whole human family and paint all of our wants with one paintbrush. That gulf is too big. Our needs however, are universal. Look at it like this; all cars are the same yet very different. A Lamborghini is a very different car from a Honda but regardless of their differences in appearance their mechanics are the same. One car may have leather interior, a turbo charged engine requiring high maintenance and the other car may have cloth interior, a fuel economic engine requiring less maintenance. Regardless of their differences, both cars need a proper mixture of *air* and *gasoline*, and the proper level of *oil* to run smoothly. It's the same with the spouse we choose. Whether they are high maintenance or low maintenance, males and females each have three basic needs. A woman's basic needs are **Security, Inspiration** and **Adoration**. A man's basic needs are **Respect, Motivation** and **Consolation**.

These three Needs of both men and women are each broken down into two categories of two great needs and one greatest need. I didn't want to say two minor needs and one major need because I didn't want the reader to minimize the importance of one iota of these needs. All of the aforementioned terms are essential to the natural makeup of the persons involved but the greatest needs give drive, motion and action. Just like oil and air are great needs of a car, all needs of the persons in a relationship are great also. The gasoline, however, is the greatest need because it is fuel that will put the vehicle in motion. Both men and women have their greatest need that is considered to be fuel also. The fuel or greatest need for the man is **Respect** and for the woman is **Security**. It is imperative for you to understand the greatest need of your partner or you will never be able to fulfill your duty, your role nor your responsibility in that relationship. When a man or woman has their greatest need met they are better able to trust, love and communicate. The trilogy of trust, love and communication will be expounded upon in Chapter 8 the Communication chapter. Let's get back to these most imperative needs of Respect and Security.

Respect for a man and Security for a woman is the most basic Need for each individual in the relationship. It's like water for a fish. It is extremely hard for a man to be in a relationship and not feel respected and it is virtually impossible for a woman to be in a relationship where she doesn't feel secure. Let's look at these two needs under a microscope and with intricacy. Let's determine why these two needs are so great and most importantly where they stem from. As the father of four, the first three are boys and the last child is a girl, I can honestly say that little girls are different. Because my daughter has three older brothers she has the ability to be rougher and less frightened than most little girls but she is still a little girl none the less.

I remember when she was about four years old; I wanted to spend time with her. No matter what I asked her, she would scream, "No"! Do you want to go to the store with daddy? "No, I want to be with Mommy"! Do you want to take a ride with daddy? "No, I want to be with Mommy"! No matter what I asked, her answer was the same. Later that night a thunderstorm rolled in and she was playing alone in her room. In an instant lightning cracked the sky, a BOOM shook the house and all of the lights went out in the whole neighborhood. In the stillness of the now pitch black house, I heard a familiar voice that wanted Mommy all day now shatter the darkness with a scream of, "DAAAD-AAAAAAAAAAY"! What was it that changed my little girl's wants into needs? Was it the lightning, the thunder or the darkness? To be honest it was neither and all of the above at the same time. It was that she now felt insecure. All children have the innate need to feel secure. This is why God blesses them with parents. Some of the duties of the parents are to nurture, teach, provide and most importantly make them feel secure. When a child feels insecure, that is usually the time when challenges with the child begin to occur such as lying. This is another subject altogether.

There is a special type of relationship between a girl and her father and a boy and his mother. In the onset the relationship between parents and children seem to be the same to one degree or another. As the children begin to grow, the relationship with the parent starts to transform in small details. Usually the boys become a little more independent and also more protective of the mother. The young man becomes protective because he sees himself growing bigger and stronger and believes his mother may not be able to protect herself the way he can protect her. The daughter also becomes more independent and protective of the father as well. She becomes protective out of respect for the one that provides her with security. So out of love for his mother, the son wants to protect his mother and make her feel secure and out of love for her father the daughter wants to protect her father because of her respect for him. What happens when the children grow up and get married? They either forget or never fully understood the impact and consequences of needs not being fulfilled such as security and respect.

Let's look at the daughter and her greatest need of security first. When a girl is at home, who is the one that makes sure all her needs are met? Who is the one that ensures her safety? Who is the one that makes sure she has a roof over her head, makes her feel safe and secure and the one she can always count on no matter what? All of these can be answered with one word, if he's living up to his responsibilities, Daddy. Why would a girl have all of this and then leave that security to get married to someone that will not make her feel secure. She won't. She assumes or would like to believe that her husband will provide her with this same level of security that her father gave her. If she doesn't have that in a father or even have her father, I guarantee it is her strongest desire. Even if she doesn't admit it, her actions will confess it.

Now let's look at the son. What is this great need of Respect for a man? When God created man and gave him dominion and authority, Respect was created to fuel the authoritative ability of the man. This is written in the very nature of the male. If the man is expected to lead, he must be fueled with respect. What CEO, general, commander, manager or supervisor will be an effective leader if those who he lead do not respect him? Even the very followers of a leader will stop following him if the leader allows himself to be disrespected. Therefore, when a boy grows older, he begins to see himself in this leadership role. If the father goes away, he *becomes* the man of the house. If he and his mom are out, he is mommy's little man and assumes the role of his father until his father returns. As he takes this role, somewhere in the back of his mind he somehow understands that respect should follow. Sometimes the mother and even the father may have to remind him who the parent is. This is a natural progression as the young man begins to assert his authority and find his way as the young leader.

One small yet powerful detail that is usually missed is that the respect a woman gives her husband creates a special love in him. Because of this love that *she* created he now *wants* to make her feel secure. In retrospect, the security a husband makes his wife feel, creates the love in her that make her *want* to give him respect. This Security, Love, Respect phenomenon is cyclical in nature. As a man makes his wife feel secure, she will continue to love him and should want to show him respect. In the same manner by the man getting this respect, he will continue to love her and will in return do whatever he has to do to make her feel secure. Just like this cyclical pattern can work for the benefit of building up a relationship, these events in reverse will work to tear down a relationship.

Let's look at a common scenario that will assist us in seeing this happen from ground level. Charles loves his wife Gloria and wants to show her how much he appreciates her by refurbishing her garden. He's working in the garden all day planting flowers so she can smell the sweet fragrance when the flowers are in full bloom. The wife sees this and decides to cook her husband's favorite meal to show him how much she appreciates him. This is simply two people in love, showing each other how much they appreciate each other. This is a beautiful scenario isn't it? When does the scenario turn for the worst?

Let's continue. The husband runs into the house to get an item he forgot. He smiles at his wife, gives her a quick smooch, throws a bag in the trash and quickly runs outside so he can finish. His wife really appreciates this little token of affection and is just as eager to finish so she can spend time with him. She notices that the trash is full but she is elbow deep in onions, bell peppers, celery and garlic. She figures since her husband is already dirty, he may not mind taking the trash out. She yells out of the kitchen window, "Hun, do you mind taking the trash out when you get a chance?" "No problem babe," he replies, "Just as soon as I can." *How can I be so lucky*, she thinks to herself and gets busy cooking? He smells that Étouffée coming from the kitchen window and thinks to himself, *Man, I love that girl; beautiful and can cook. How can I be so lucky?* At this point they are both toiling to please one another.

"Dinner is ready", she yells through the window. He gathers all of his tools and runs to take a quick shower because he knows how much she likes for them eat dinner together. "I'll be right out, he yells from the shower. After his shower and he gets dressed and steps to the dinner table wearing her favorite cologne. She's just as dazzling wearing his

77

favorite outfit. She notices how handsome he is and says, "Aw babe, I didn't want you to have to mess with that dirty trash can after you showered", she says with a wink. "Don't worry about that", he replies. "I'll get it after dinner." The romance goes on from dinner until late.

The next morning he runs out before she gets up to take care of a few things. She jumps up after she remembers she has a house showing today. When she gets back, he is just finishing the lawn and walks into the house to greet her. She puts her briefcase down and jokingly says, "I'll fix us some lunch if you don't forget the trash again." Exhausted, he softly says, "I said I'll get it baby girl. Just let me catch my breath." In his mind he's thinking, *Here we go again. Nag, nag, nag; talking to me like I'm a child again. I knew it wouldn't last. I knew it was too good to be true. I'm gonna just tell her I forgot I was supposed to meet Rob today. I'll just go get a beer and shoot some pool somewhere.* She says in her sweetest voice, "I know you will hun. It's just a friendly reminder." In her mind she says, *Man, I cook, I clean, I go to work and then cook again. Why do I constantly have to keep asking this man to do things for me over and over again? Anyone else and he's Johnny on the spot. Am I that unimportant to him? If he says he has somewhere to go, I'm going to explode. Every time it looks like we're about to have a disagreement, he has somewhere to go. He never wants to face anything. I can't take this up and down anymore.* The ticking of the clock on the wall is the only audible sound until he finally says, "Man, I forgot I was supposed to meet Rob this afternoon." Immediately she says with a low cold tone, "I'm gonna have to give Rob my wedding ring as much time as you two spend together." His low, "Humph" is the only thing that breaks the silence as he walks towards the shower.

How did this scenario go wrong? Remember both parties were aiming to please the other in the beginning. He was planting flowers for her and she was cooking his favorite meal. They were both determined to give the advantage to each other. As soon as a portion of the covenant began to be threatened, the weeds of discontentment started to surface and the two greatest needs began to become violated. In this instance it was gradual and almost unnoticeable. In other instances it can be sudden and even violent but what was the threat? Remember the greatest need of a man is Respect and the greatest need of a woman is Security. Although the trash seems to be the catalyst in this scenario, it was only the spark that ignited the powder keg that has been brewing.

It would seem that Gloria and Charles have a history of this type of behavior. In the beginning it looked like they were just trying to show each other how much they loved and appreciated the other. It turns out that it was just an attempt to put a band aid on a wound that has been festering for some time now. The real issue is that Charles and Gloria's greatest Needs have not been met. At this time we do not know who started neglecting the Need first or how it even began. At this point, it really doesn't matter. Now, they need to simply understand that it *is* happening. When Gloria kept dropping little hints to Charles about the trash, Charles thought she started treating him like a child. The minute he *thought* his wife was looking at him as a child, he *feels* she no longer sees him as a man. As a result he feels disrespected. Anger starts to build within him and he wants to avoid another conflict or avoid saying something he will regret, so he leaves. When he leaves, she sees him as withdrawing from her wondering who or what is he being drawn to. She now *feels* that she may be losing him to something or someone else. She now feels insecure.

The scenario may change but the circumstances are normally the same. The woman feels insecure and the man feels disrespected. If a wife finds a phone number in her husband's pocket, the argument that is sure to follow will not be about the number, she now somehow feels insecure. If she gets on him about unnecessary spending, she feels financially insecure. If she makes a big deal about him staying out a little late or not calling when he is late, she feels insecure. It's the same way with a man. If his wife approaches him with an accusatory tone, he feels disrespected. If he is questioned about buying a new hammer, he feels disrespected. If he just wants to hang out with the guys and his wife complains, he feels disrespected. Anytime a man feels that someone else (especially his wife) doesn't look at him as a man, he feels disrespected and anytime a woman feels that her well being, the well being of her family or her home is threatened, she feels insecure.

As long as a man loves his wife and makes her feel secure, she will usually reciprocate that love and honor him with respect. This is cyclical in nature as long as both parties purpose in their hearts and make a commitment that they're going to give their spouse what they *need*. This is why in Ephesians Chapter 5, Paul tells the wives to submit to their husbands as unto the Lord, not like she is a pet and he is her master but as one who understands that he is the head. Since the man is the head, esteem, honor and respect him in the same manner as the church honors Christ as its head. This will solidify his authoritativeness and enable him in being the head and he will begin to fulfill all of his wife's needs. Paul then gives wisdom to men to love their wives as Christ loves the church. Paul says that husband's relationship with their wives ought to mimic Christ's relationship with the church. He said that Christ sacrificed himself for the church. Christ leading and being the head of the church is for the benefit of the church, not of himself. By doing this the church becomes glorious or radiant. Once husbands provide and care for their wives physically, mentally, spiritually and emotionally, the wives will become glorious, radiant, youthful and girlish, because they have been made to feel secure.

Now that we've discussed our greatest Needs of Security and Respect, let's discuss our great Needs of <u>Inspiration</u> and <u>Adoration</u> for a woman and <u>Motivation</u> and <u>Consolation</u> for a man. Everyone needs to be inspired or motivated. One of the greatest gifts a person can possess is the ability to inspire or motivate others to achieve their own greatness. This special talent is what makes CEO's, pastors, coaches and other great leaders relevant. They are able to inspire and motivate. They are able to make others see an ability within themselves to do greater than they thought they could. You can pick any CEO that is extremely savvy in negotiations and financial transactions or a football coach that is supremely efficient in strategy and play calling, if they aren't able to inspire and motivate, their talents will be wasted in the profession they are in. The hardest thing for a person to do is the simplest task they'll have to achieve; that is to simply get started. People will plan, map out and sometimes go through great lengths to prepare to do some great undertaking and then will never get started because they were not inspired or motivated.

Inspiration and motivation are each a greater need of women and men respectively. They're not the greatest need but a great need none the less. Women need to be inspired and men need to be motivated. These two words, inspire and motivate are so closely related in definition that they are almost interchangeable. The difference lies not in the definition

81

but in the very act itself. The act of inspiration usually involves someone doing something first and then the other person being moved and compelled by what they see and desiring to achieve the same effect. Motivation on the other hand requires more of a cheerleader type incitement. When a man hears his wife say, "You can do it" or "If no one else believes in you, I do!" or if a woman hears her husband say, "I believe in you." That is like putting jet fuel in his or her engine. After that, nothing will be able to stop them. Everyone needs a little push every once in a while. Some may not need it as much as others but the *need* is still there.

Two additional great needs for women and men are Adoration and Consolation respectively. These two needs are no less important than the previous ones. As a matter of fact they complement the previous. When a woman consoles her husband, she is giving him *peace of mind*. There is no man that can admit that he does not function better when the home is in order or when he is able to be tranquil in his thoughts. Not only does he feel respected when his mate goes out of her way to console him but he is also motivated to do more around the house and beyond. In retrospect, when a woman feels that she is adored by her husband, she feels like she is *the most beautiful woman* walking on the planet and all women want and *need* to feel this way. When a man makes his wife feel beautiful and adored, she has no reason to feel insecure about anything. She is also inspired to do more for him as well as herself because she understands that this soothing of his mind will in return generate more adoration for her.

If each person in the marriage would make an attempt to at least meet their spouse's basic *needs*, of security, inspiration and adoration for a woman and respect, motivation and consolation for a man, many of the issues that couples face would be eradicated immediately. Now, what needs to be done is find out what those three things mean to your spouse. Security for one wife may mean something totally different to another but she needs security none the less. Respect may be defined as something totally different by two different husbands but respect will still be his greatest need. By truly understanding the greater and greatest needs of your spouse, countless hours of explaining why certain needs aren't being met would be eliminated. It will also increase the joyous occasions of *getting* your needs met. These set of needs; both greatest and great far outweighs *wants* in any arena. Also, remember, if wants ever outweigh needs, WATCHOUT! Hell and Havoc are sure to follow.

The Basic Needs of a Woman:

Security-Inspiration and Adoration

The Basic NEEDS of a Man:

Respect-Motivation and Consolation.

Do I really understand my Spouse's Greatest NEED and am I doing all I can to fulfill both their greater and greatest needs?

What am I doing to ensure that I am fulfilling those needs?

~7~

Roles and Responsibilities

Ephesians 5:22-25
Wives, submit to your own husbands, as to the Lord. 23 For the husband is head of the wife, as also Christ is head of the church; and He is the Savior of the body. 24 Therefore, just as the church is subject to Christ, so let the wives be to their own husbands in everything. 25 Husbands, love your wives, just as Christ also loved the church and gave Himself for her,

This is the chapter I expect to get the most flack. If what is said in this chapter doesn't pertain to you, then it shouldn't affect you. It has been my experience that people tend to avoid getting into conversations of defining roles for one of three reasons or fall into one of three categories: failure to understand their role, disbelief in a need of roles, or refusal to accept responsibility of a role. The first two reasons are reasonable to understand because of a lack of awareness. However, it is the third reason that is most dangerous and detrimental to marriage. Those that fall in the first two categories can still be taught. Those that fall in the latter category are aware of the role of a wife and a husband but simply don't want to fulfill that responsibility. They use words like ancient, archaic or old fashioned to describe roles. They may even say things like, "That was good in the 30's, 40's or 50's, maybe even the 60's but NOT today. This is the 21st century." Why was it good in the 30's, 40's, 50's and MAYBE even the 60's? What major event took place in the 60's and had definitely changed by the 1970's that roles of men and women became archaic? We'll discuss this and hit that nail on the head in a few seconds but let's determine if roles are still valid.

Let's say that my wife is a power lifter and I'm one that does not exercise or lifts weights, ever. Naturally, she may be bigger and stronger than I am but there is still an order to nature. If we're lying in bed at night and I hear a noise in the backyard, I am not going to wake my wife and whisper, "Baby, I hear something in the backyard. Are **you** gonna go check it out?" Knowing my wife like I do, she would probably look at me as if to say, "If I have to go check it out, *why* in the 'snap beans' did I marry *you*!" and she would be correct. Although, she is bigger and stronger than I am, it is neither her role nor her responsibility and she knows this. Right now many of you who are reading this may not believe in roles and may want to ascertain that my example lacks merit. You may not want to admit that it isn't her role but you will have to agree that it isn't her responsibility. Let's look a little closer and see why most people have issues with roles.

Many people have issues with roles innocently enough because they confuse roles with tasks. Going to check on the noise in the backyard isn't necessarily a *role* as much as it is a *task* but in this instance it is the task that defines the role. This task should be fulfilled by the one whose responsibility it is to provide security. Remember, the greatest need of a woman *is* security. Well, if my wife's *need* is security, then fulfilling that *need* is my responsibility. We must admit that for me not to fulfill my role and to allow my wife to perform *my* role would simply frustrate her as a woman. It has to be seen that frustration is also at the core of many failed marriages. Frustration occurs because a need isn't being met and the need isn't being met because a role isn't being filled. Let's just look at the word *frustrate* and then talk about *tasks*.

Frustrate - 1. a. To **prevent from accomplishing a purpose** or fulfilling a desire; to thwart. b. To cause feelings of **discouragement** or bafflement in. 2. To make ineffectual or invalid; nullify. 3. To upset or agitate.

Looking back at the last four chapters we can see how frustration can enter a relationship. First, in Chapter 3, we determined the purpose of marriage. It is not only to get assistance but more importantly to *give* assistance to my mate in fulfilling their God given purpose. If that assistance isn't being given, frustration is likely to occur. Chapter 4 talked about making the transitions from dating to courting and from courting to matrimony. It also talks about how during the courting phase that all aspects of the relationship should be taken into consideration, put on trial and then make a determination if this current relationship will result in a productive marriage. If all questions aren't answered and a clear understanding of what is expected is established, again frustration will likely occur. Chapter 5 basically determines that what most people call love or that emotional high they get from the opposite sex is just that, an *emotional* high. Therefore, this emotional high shouldn't have much validity in the decision making process toward marriage because usually when the feelings vanish, so does the relationship. When that emotional high is gone and the relationship has no substance, frustration will occur. Chapter 6 brought a lot of things into perspective. It gave insight to the needs and desires of men and women. It determined that the greatest need for a woman is security and the greatest need for a man is respect.

We must conclude that if we can't see ourselves receiving our greatest need from our potential spouse and us reciprocating, then we must make a hard yet calculated decision. We may not be ready to move forward into matrimony. We have already established that when needs aren't being met, frustrations will occur.

I now challenge you, the reader, to see and understand that as a mate it is our responsibility to meet the needs of our spouses. The only way we will fulfill our responsibility is if we accept our *role* in the marriage. Notice, I didn't say relationship. A marriage unlike a relationship is a covenant and a bond. You can get out of a relationship without any problems because you aren't legally bound by law. A marriage, on the other hand, is a bond and you are bound by a covenant. At this point I have to add that many people live together and actually think they are in a covenant relationship. If a relationship ends and property and family has to be divided and the couple is not married, then there *is* no covenant. Simply put, they were 'playing house'. This may be hard for some to swallow but it still needs to be said. House play is another reason there are so many failed marriages. Too many married people played house and when they *finally* decided to get married, they didn't treat the marriage any different. First of all, who do you expect to 'play house' other than children? When children play house, the boy *acts* like a man and wants to get the same respect and *benefits* of a loving husband and father. The girl *acts* like a woman and wants to get the same treatment and *benefits* of a devoted wife and mother. They both want the benefits but not necessarily want to *commit* to the *responsibility* of the *role* they are *playing*. Neither *child* truly made a commitment to the other so when the *children* don't get their way, they say, "I quit! I'm going home." Then she takes her dolls and he takes his marbles and they both go play something with someone else. That's why 1 Corinthians 13:11 says, *"When I was a child, I spoke as a child* (**why**), (because) *I understood as a child* (**why**), (because) *I thought as a child:* (**what happened when you became mature**) *but when I became a man, I put away childish things."*

Let's get back to roles. As stated earlier, most people who do not like to define roles in marriage are the same people who shy away from their responsibilities. Oftentimes, we don't want to fulfill our roles because we get roles confused with tasks. *Tasks* and *roles* are two entirely different things. Roles are made up of our core attributes of who we are, how God made us and for what purpose. Tasks are the things that we do. This is why people say that roles were acceptable during the 30's, 40's and 50's. During the 1960's is when industry began to change and a full blown sexual revolution emerged during the 1970's. Our tasks began to mesh together and then they became blurred. Women could no longer be relegated to the *tasks* of the home such as cooking, cleaning, taking care of the children, doing the laundry and other household chores. The men were no longer the sole bread winners of the family because the husband and the wife both began to work outside of the home. The family heads began to share the burden of making the family financially stable but the *tasks* remained and gradually became unclear. The more people worked the greater gains they made. As they made greater gains, their wants became greater. Education was pursued even more to make even more gains in income to keep up with greater wants and desires. This greater education made women more financially independent. Wives began to make as much money as their husbands and sometimes even more which made them the primary bread winner.

If she becomes the primary breadwinner or if her salary becomes equal to her husband's or even depended upon, confusion will most likely occur. Chaos will be sure to follow if either party is confusing roles with tasks. The wife wants to know why she has do most of the housework when she is working outside of the home as well. The husband wants to know why his wife isn't being submissive like women used to be back in the 'good ole days'. She becomes frustrated because somewhere in the back of her mind she feels that he is not taking care of his responsibility by taking care of her. If he was, then she wouldn't have to work so hard outside of the home as well as inside of the home. He's frustrated because he's been at work all day (if he can find a job) and still has to come home and clean the house. The most frustrating part for him is that he has to deal with nagging and attitude while he's doing it. What the couple may not understand is that there may be a valid reason for the verbalized frustrations. Until they get to the core of their frustrations, they will only become more frustrated because of the underlying issues.

As stated before in an earlier chapter, the most important question a person can ever ask himself is 'why'. Why is there so much frustration and where is it coming from? The answer is simple. There is a misunderstanding of roles, scripture and of the very nature of men and women. Let's make sense of this and bring balance to where there is an imbalance. We'll start with the misunderstanding of scripture first. Since God is the creator and manufacturer of all things, who is better than the manufacturer himself to explain to us his design and product. Let's attempt to understand scripture and see if it doesn't clear up the rest of the confusion. Now, since the man was created first, let's deal with him.

*23 For the husband is **head** of the wife, as also Christ is head of the church; and He is the Savior of the body. 24 Therefore, just as the church is **subject** to Christ, so let the wives be to their own husbands in everything.* **Ephesians 5:23, 24**

Ephesians Chapter 5 says that the husband is the head of the wife as Christ is the head of the church. It goes on to say that the church is Christ's body, he sacrificed himself for it and that husbands should do likewise for their wives. It also says that as the church is subject to Christ, so should the wives be subject to their own husbands. What is quite interesting is that Paul uses the metaphors of husband, Christ and head. He also uses the metaphors of wife, church and body. Before we analyze this lets deal with the words *subject* and *head* before the young female reader throws this book in the trash or the young man shoves it in her face saying, "See, it's written right here!"

The word "subject" is taken from the Greek, military term *Hupotasso* which means to arrange in military fashion under a commander. Outside of the military, it means a *voluntary attitude* of giving in, yielding to and cooperating with. This is something worthy enough to slow down and analyze or the crucial point may be missed or misrepresented. Ephesians 5:23 says, *the husband is head of the wife, as also Christ is head of the church; and He is the Savior of the body.* The *head* is the part that has been designated as the *maintainer* of the body. It ensures that the body is nourished and functions to its fullest capacity. It is through the head that the body is protected from sickness and disease insuring that the body is *secure* and *protected.* The head uses acquired *knowledge* and implements *wisdom* to direct and guide the body and ensure that it doesn't go through any undue stress or harm. Because the body understands that the head is there to lead, guide and maintain it, it submits willingly. It understands that there are no hidden agendas or motives. The body also knows and understands that all decisions made by the head will be made to benefit the entire body and not just the head itself or certain members. It must also be said right here that not only is the wife a part of the body but the children are also members of that same body. Therefore the body submits willingly and is at peace and harmony with itself and those around it. Let's look at the other side of the coin. What if there is a person with a well developed brain that is able to lead yet the body does not submit? It would be said that person is paralyzed or has some type of physical affliction. What if the body is willing to submit but the brain is unable or unwilling to lead? This person would be said to be in a vegetated state or have some form of mental deficiency.

This is how it is in some of our homes. The husband has the capacity to lead but the wife or even the family is either unwilling or unable to follow. How about if the wife is ready to follow but her husband is unable to lead? This too connotes some type of affliction. Looking a little deeper, what if the church claimed to love Christ but refused to submit to Him for whatever reason? Then the body doesn't truly love the head and a false claim of love as been expressed. Also, what if Christ was unwilling or incapable of leading the church? The church could make the claim that she has chosen an unworthy leader. Neither situation would be harmonious for the well being of the unit as a whole or the relationship itself.

Sometimes there is a reason that the head will not lead the body and the body will not submit to the head. If we remember our last chapter, the greatest need of a woman is security and the greatest need of a man is respect. A man is more apt to lead his family if he is feeling respected and a woman is more willing to submit to her husband if she is feeling secure. Let's look at scripture and see if this is true.

¹ Now the LORD had said to Abram: "Get out of your country, From your family And from your father's house, To a land that I will show you. **Gen 12:1**

⁴ So Abram departed as the LORD had spoken to him, and Lot went with him. And Abram was seventy-five years old when he departed from Haran. **Gen 12:4**

Now, here is God, Abram's head, attempting to lead and guide him to a greater place from where he has been. Abram *should* willingly submit to the authority and head of his life. Many people think he did but he only partially submitted. God told Abram to leave his family and Abram, thinking he is doing a good thing, decides to bring his nephew Lot with him. It's understandable why Abram did this. He was looking out for the best interest of his nephew but it went against what the head of his life directed him to do. Because Abram did not respect the authority or head of his life that authority now refuse to lead him. If you notice God, the head, only said one short sentence to Abram while Lot was with him. When Abram passed through Canaan in verse 12 of that same chapter all God said was, "To your descendents, I will give this Land." That was it! There were no great details, no boundaries, no direction or leadership. Respect and submission was not entirely given to the head, so the head did not lead. Yes, He kept providing and protecting Abram but he didn't take on that complete role of leader because his role as head was not respected.

This is how it is in many of our homes. If the husband doesn't feel respected or that he is the head, he may continue to provide and protect but may not take on the role of leader. If the wife insists on being the head in every area of the relationship, he questions, "Well, what do I need to do it for? Apparently she has it." This will begin to eat at the very core of the man. He may begin to detach himself from the role of headship and possibly from the family itself. He may start to die to himself and become a shell of a man. She will never be fully satisfied with him in that capacity and will eventually begin to despise him. He may begin to fall so far away from his role and responsibilities that he may allow someone else to take his attention and give him the respect he *feels* he deserves.

Now what if there is a husband that has a wife that wants to submit but he is unwilling or unable to take on the leadership role? Eventually, it will be hard for her to continue to submit and that feeling of insecurity will eventually take over. Let's look at our example in Rehoboam, Solomon's son, the new king of Israel, and Israel herself. In this instance, the body wanted to subject itself to the head but couldn't.

¹ And Rehoboam went to Shechem, for **all Israel** *had gone to Shechem* **to make him king***. Then Jeroboam and the whole assembly of Israel came and spoke to Rehoboam, saying, ⁴ "Your father made our yoke heavy; now therefore, lighten the burdensome service of your father, and his heavy yoke which he put on us, and* **we will serve you***."1Kings 12:1-4*

Here is a king that has a kingdom and a people that want to submit and be loyal to him. They come to him with reasonable requests. They wanted to treat him like a king and submit themselves to him. All they asked for their loyalty and submission was for him to deal *fairly* with them. Rehoboam wasn't sure how to handle this so he sought out counsel. If you would read further, you would see that he went to the wise elders first and the elders advised him to meet the people's request and deal justly with them. They told him that if he dealt justly with them, the people would be loyal to him for his entire kingship. Apparently that answer wasn't good enough because he next sought out the advice of his childhood friends (those that knew no more than he did). His friends basically told him to tell the people that he was the king of his castle and that he was not only going to be as hard as his father but even harder. Let's see how that turned out for him.

16 Now when all Israel saw that the king did not listen to them, the people answered the king, saying: "What share have we in David? We have no inheritance in the son of Jesse. To your tents, O Israel! Now, see to your own house, O David!" **1Kings 12:16**

The people said that since the king refused to lead and maintain the *body*, then they will have to be responsible for themselves. Even though there was a head in place for the body, it refused to submit. They didn't' refuse because the body was disobedient or the head was not there but because the head refused to lead and deal justly with them. If this is the case, then the body is now left feeling unloved and uncared for. As a result, they felt responsible for themselves and led their own houses. This is the way it is in many marriages today. Many men don't know or understand their role as the husband and leader of their homes. Many wives don't know or understand their role as a wife. People are confusing roles with tasks. This is bringing more confusion in the homes and a greater level of frustration. This gradual rise in frustration is a direct reflection of the gradual rise in the divorce rate.

So what are the roles of the husband and wife? Paul, who was never married, used the two greatest relationships that he was familiar with to describe the roles between husband and wife. He uses Christ and Church and head and body. In Ephesians Chapter 5 he writes:

22 **Wives,** *submit* **to your own husbands,** *as to the Lord. 23 For the husband is* **head** *of the wife, as also* **Christ** *is head of the* **church***; and He is the Savior of the* **body***. 24 Therefore, just as the* **church** *is subject to* **Christ***, so let the* **wives** *be to* *their own* **husbands** *in everything.* [25] **Husbands,** **love your wives,** *just as* **Christ** *also loved the* **church** *and gave Himself for her the* **body***(mine),* **Ephesians 5:22-25**

The metaphor Paul uses in this scripture illustrates the role of husband to wife and wife to husband. The role of husband should be that of a leader. If one looks at the characteristics of an effective leader, certain attributes usually come to mind: impartial yet decisive, strong yet compassionate, wise yet understanding, fearless yet sensitive, serious yet light-hearted and humble yet exemplary. These are the attributes of one of the best leaders I ever had the opportunity of following while in the military. If a woman would be honest, these are also the attributes she would choose for her husband if she could. These are also the attributes of Christ if one would look closely and actually think about it. He was the epitome of strength yet the most humble man that ever lived. He judged fairly and impartially over all. He was fearless in the face of death and had the wisdom of God yet was understanding and sensitive to weaknesses of all those that followed him. Christ was the greatest example a man could ever have of being a husband to his wife because he loved the church, took the lead in everything and even sacrificed himself to the death for her. Likewise a husband should love, lead and sacrifice his life for his wife and family as well.

Once this awesome task is taken on by the head to lead and take the 'full' responsibility of the body or the family, an enormous amount of pressure and stress is placed on the head or the mind of the leader. The body should be there to support the head and also console the mind of the leader. If we remember in the previous chapter, consolation is one of the greater needs of the man. Consolation is a natural ability of a woman. If she chooses to use this gift is another story. Notice, when one woman is going through a tough time in her life, her girlfriends or other women comes to her aid to comfort and console her. They may not offer advice nor give solutions. Simply being there and relieving some of the pressure by their God given talents offers consolation. Think of how effective a wife can give consolation to her husband's stressed mind. It would be more beneficial than a beer or his hours of flipping channels on TV. Nothing outside of God himself can relieve a husband's weary mind than the consolation of his wife. It gives him *peace* when he sees her manifested desire to bring consolation and comfort to his stressed and weary mind. Likewise, nothing outside of God himself will make a wife feel more secure than knowing that she has a husband that loves her and will sacrifice his everything to ensure that she is safe, secure and taken care of.

We could go on and on about this chapter because there is so much to it. We must come to a stopping point but we will attempt to surmise all that has been said. Paul uses the metaphors of Christ and church, husband and wife and head and body. Let's get a thorough deduction using the symbolism of head and body. As stated earlier, the head is the part that leads the rest of the body. It directs the body with wisdom and guides it so that it will be maintained and relieved of any undue stress. It maintains and upkeeps the body so that it will perform at its optimum level. This is the same type of maintenance that is performed on a home or any other object that a person may regard as special and desire to be kept for a long time. Only in this particular instance, this item should be maintained not only with wisdom but also with love and understanding. This is the role of the husband which is leader. The responsibility of the head is to ensure that the greater needs of the body are met. Remember the greater needs of the body are security, inspiration and adoration. If the body receives the greater needs at a minimum, the head is fulfilling his responsibility.

On the other hand, the body has the obligation of supporting the head. The body has the unique ability to relieve the head as well as sustain it with its needs. The body pushes oxygen up to the head from the lungs thereby nourishing the brain and then draws the depleted blood away from the brain which will in turn relieve it of unnecessary pressure. The same goes for the wife with her husband. The wife has the unique ability to speak into her husband's life and build him up like no other person can. She has the ability to feed and nourish his self-esteem like the lungs feeds the brain with oxygen. This much needed breathe of life will give the brain and the husband to ability to think clearly, be innovative, inventive, enabling and giving him the desire to lead his family properly. She also has the ability to relieve unnecessary pressure from her husband's weary mind by consoling and soothing him. This refreshes and rejuvenates him so he is able to go out and lead again tomorrow. This is the role of the wife as the strength and support of the leader. The responsibility that falls under this role is accomplished by giving the husband his greater needs which are respect, motivation and consolation.

If both parties gave their partners their greater needs at a minimum, they will be fulfilling their roles and accepting their responsibilities. By accepting and fulfilling their roles and responsibilities, couples have the ability to single handedly raise the success rate of their own marriage and maintain that success rate throughout their relationship.

Do I fully understand what my role is and what my responsibilities are?

Question, am I fully accepting my role and fulfilling my responsibility.

~8~

The Meeting of Two Nations
(The Art of Effective Communication)

Ephesians 4:29
Let no corrupt communication proceed out of your mouth, but that which is good to the use of edifying, that it may minister grace unto the hearers.

If couples get an understanding of their roles and responsibilities, their wants, needs and desires, what love actually is and even the purpose of marriage, it will all count for nothing if this particular chapter isn't understood and implemented. Two people fighting side by side to save their marriage is no different than two people or two combat units fighting side by side in warfare. Being an old combat soldier, I understand all too well the rules of engagement. The first thing that must be understood is that you just don't launch an all out attack against a superior force without some preconditioning. Notice, I said a superior force. Regardless of what you believe, that's what your marriage is compared to its enemy; a Superior Force. If a smaller unit attempts a full blown attack against a larger and stronger force, the weaker unit would not have the resources to overwhelm the larger force and therefore would be overwhelmed themselves and would surely approach sudden death with an all out attack.

The easiest way for a smaller or weaker force to win a battle over a stronger or more superior force is to antagonize, confuse and disrupt before attempting to dismantle their enemy with an all out attack. To antagonize your superior force, the enemy will send out little, small two to three man units that will make "hit and run" pop shots against your unit from different angles. This is designed to thin your forces because you really won't know where the next attack may be coming from so you will have to send more people out to guard your perimeter. Depending on the level of a certain required skill set, which we'll mention shortly, these pop shots will either strengthen or confuse your unit. If this skill set is high, your unit will make proper adjustments and then defend your unit without over utilizing its resources. If this certain skill set is low, you will shift from being antagonized to confused and eventually your whole operation will be in disarray. Once your operations are disrupted it is only a matter of time before your unit is being dismantled by your enemy with an all out attack. This is inevitable once a weakness in your unit has been discovered.

This skill set that was mentioned earlier is one that must be strengthened and hardened. It is the ability to communicate. The law of combat says that the very first resource the enemy will make an attack on is your communications. If you have no communication or if your communication skills are soft and weak, your enemy has already defeated you and you don't even know it. With all that you have, be it money, prestige, sex, good looks or what have you, you are just prolonging the inevitable, which is the demise of your marriage.

What is communication? According to Webster, communication is derived from the word communicate which means:

Communication - *To convey knowledge or information; to transmit information, thought, or feeling so that it is satisfactorily received or understood*

The first part of the Webster's definition is *to convey knowledge or information*. This partial meaning of communication is the part we have the least amount of difficulty with. Very few people have an issue with conveying. When you convey all you're doing is really passing on information or telling someone something such as how you feel. Many times this is the sum total of what we actually perceive communication to be. We're not worried about how what we say may be received. We don't worry about if it makes sense or even if it will offend the recipient of the message. What we really want is to be heard or ensure that our point is *conveyed* regardless of how it was received or perceived. Even in a conversation, we may not be worried of how our message is coming across to others and we sometimes are not actively listening to what the other person is saying. We in fact may listen just enough to refute what is being said or seeking an opportunity or opening where we can *convey* our own piece of information. In itself, *conveying* isn't communication but rather a half hearted attempt to communicate. It is only a portion of communication and very little of this portion will prove to be a healthy benefit to any type of relationship.

The second part of that definition is: *to **transmit** information, thought, or feeling so that it is **satisfactorily received** or **understood.*** The last portion of the definition is a tad bit different from the first part of the definition. The first part of the definition is to simply ***convey*** *knowledge or information*. A man on a desert island can convey information. He can write a note, stick it in a bottle and toss the bottle into the ocean and hope that someone will eventually read it. Yes, he conveyed knowledge or information but he didn't *transmit* knowledge or information. When you transmit however, you are looking for that knowledge or information, according to the definition; to be *satisfactorily received or understood.* I humbly submit to you that if the information is not understood, it will hardly be satisfactorily received. Now, in the scientific world there are two things needed for proper transmission; a transmitter and a receiver and the more sophisticated the equipment is, the more reliable the communication will be. With sophisticated equipment the transmitter will first send out a signal that the receiver can decipher or understand. The receiver must then decipher or make sense of that signal and then acknowledge to the receiver that the signal has been properly sent, or in the case of our definition, satisfactorily received.

What happens when the transmitter and the receiver are operating on two different frequencies or with different types of signals? They are unable to communicate. The transmitter is attempting to transmit and the receiver is attempting to receive but there is no communication going on because they are unable to understand the other's language. As a result, there is a break in communication. In the case of equipment, a converter or translator must be placed between the two device's signals to convert or translate the signal so that the other may be able to decode or understand what is being transmitted or said.

The same thing takes place in our relationships. People may be communicating effectively for a time and then all of a sudden they begin to have communication issues. It's like having a computer that has been working fine and all of a sudden it's having issues communicating with one of its devices. One of two things has happened. Either new software has been introduced to the computer or one of the pieces that is being used to communicate is starting to malfunction. Regardless of the issue, communication must be restored in order for the equipment to work properly. In the case of new software being introduced to the system, it is like when one partner gets a new way of looking at something or a new way of thinking. He or she may start communicating differently. When this partner gets this new epiphany, the other partner may still attempt to communicate the way they used to and in the words of Dr. Phil, "That dog won't hunt." There is now a break in communication. Something now has to be placed between the two devices that can now assist in decoding the coded language so that the two can once again be able to communicate. What happens to a computer that can't communicate with its hard drive or CD ROM? You either take it somewhere to get fixed or look at it uselessly sitting on the desk and get more disgusted as time goes by. Eventually you'll just throw it away becoming even more disgusted than before because you let it sit around so long just taking up space. The first thing you should do is attempt to get it fixed as soon as you see possible issues. In this instance, it can possibly be saved along with some valuable information you have on there. The longer you wait, the more your chances increase of losing some valuable information.

This is all well and good learning about computers and other electronic equipment but how does this compare to marriage and relationships? The exact same process happens with people and relationships as alluded to earlier. Some people have been in a relationship and have never been able to truly communicate. Others have been in a relationship and were able to communicate effectively at one time until some traumatic event or experience occurs. Once the event takes place, they are never able to communicate as effectively as they use to. Something or someone must now be placed in between 'these' two devices or persons that can now assist in the decoding of each other's language. If someone isn't placed in between them to assist them, detriment to the relationship will surely follow. Let's replay a popular event by pulling out a few scriptures to see if there is any relevance to what is being said.

The Tower of Babel

Genesis 11:1, 4, 6, 7, 8

1) *¹ And the whole earth* **was of one language,** *and* **of one speech.** **Gen:11:1**
   ❖ It is possible to have positive and *effective* communication.

2) *⁴ And they said, Go to,* **let us build us a city and a tower, whose top may reach unto heaven;** *and let us make us a name, lest we be scattered abroad upon the face of the whole earth.* **Gen:11:4**
   ❖ People with effective communications can accomplish great and extraordinary things.

3) *⁶ And the* LORD *said, Behold,* **the people is one, and they have all one language;** *and this they begin to do: and now* **nothing will be restrained from them,** *which they have imagined to do.* **Gen:11:6**
   ❖ When people have positive communications, there is nothing they cannot achieve and others notice it.

4) *⁷ Go to, let us go down, and there* **confound their language, that they may not understand one another**'s *speech.* **Gen:11:7**
   ❖ Usually it is some experience or event that hinders effective communication.

5) *⁸ So the* LORD **scattered them abroad** *from thence upon the face of all the earth: and they* **left off (or ceased) to build the city. Gen:11:8** (Words in parentheses are mine).
   ❖ When people are unable to communicate, they usually separate either physically or mentally and are unable to be productive in their relationships and even in the building of their plans.

Many relationships are like the Tower of Babel. It starts out where everyone involved are not only speaking the same language but are also speaking as one or conveying the same thoughts and ideas. The relationship is beautiful in the beginning because we are speaking the same language of love and excitement. We have these wonderful ideas that we bounce off of one another and we feel like together we can do anything. We feel that together we can conquer the world. We make these grand plans for our own lives and other people may even see that spark or glimmer in our eyes confirming for us that we can do it. We are on top of the world and planning to go even higher until BAM! Something has changed and we realize that we are no longer speaking the same language. Now, we can no longer work together because, like at the tower of Babel, we can no longer understand one another.

As in the Tower of Babel some traumatic experience, such as infidelity, can have this immediate effect where all of a sudden we no longer speak the same language. It can all be a strain for the triangle of love, trust and communication. What has happened is our love has now been questioned, we now don't trust one another and it will be just as hard to believe one another. Now since we no longer are able to understand one another, we are no longer able to communicate. This can be the effects of distrust in communications.

The Tower of Babel story is an example of a quick and immediate change in languages. What others may see is not the immediate change in communications but rather the gradual and subtle change that is described in 24th chapter of Proverbs:

*[30]I once walked by the field and the vineyard of a lazy fool. [31]Thorns and weeds were everywhere, **and the stone wall had fallen down**. [32]When I saw this, it taught*

me a lesson: [33]*Sleep a little. Doze a little. Fold your hands and twiddle your thumbs.*
[34]*(and it seems as if) Suddenly poverty hits you and everything is gone!* **Proverbs 24:30-34 (CEV)**

This passage says that someone went by the field and vineyard of a slothful or lazy person. In this particular passage the person is described as being a fool, not because of the position he finds himself but more so because of how he allowed himself to be put into this position. If read carefully it says that thorns and weeds were everywhere AND the stone wall had fallen down. This alludes to the fact that this vineyard wasn't always like this and has now become overrun with corruption because of negligence. If you have the slightest inkling of farming you know that weeds will not just spring up in one day. Weeds come up so slow that it is hardly noticeable. Owners may painstakingly pull weeds to clean up their gardens at a particular time and then feel that they can relax a little because all is well on the surface. The few sprigs coming up are hardly noticeable and don't really require that much attention. People feel they can wait until tomorrow but tomorrow often becomes next week and next week becomes a few months. Before you know it, your garden is overgrown with weeds again. In the case of this passage, it seems that the owner took such a long break that even the stone wall he built to protect the garden came down. The stone wall coming down is profound in itself and will be discussed in the next chapter of adultery.

The slow process of a break in communication is an appropriate fit for this parable. When people are in relationships and have effective communications, they may become complacent and feel that they don't have to put in as much effort as they use to. They may feel their communication is effective enough at the time. When one person begins to perceive an idea *slightly* different than their partner and it is not at least

109

understood *why*, confusion will soon take place. No matter how minor it may seem, it is at this time the soft stemmed weed of misunderstanding will begin to push its way through the ground of communication. This is usually unbeknownst to the parties involved. Because it's a small and soft stem, it is not perceived as such big deal so we'll just put it on the backburner until later, if we deal with it at all. When one stem of difference starts to sprout and push its delicate head through the tough soil, others are sure to follow. If not dealt with immediately or as the passage puts it, *"[33]Sleep a little. Doze a little. Fold your hands and twiddle your thumbs. [34]* **(and it seems as if) Suddenly** *poverty hits you."* This poverty will surely be the brokenness of your communication, your relationship or eventually your marriage and it will seem as if it hit you all of a sudden. In reality, it was a slow and almost unnoticeable process. I say almost unnoticeable because we notice and see the changes but like the owner of the vineyard, we sit idle and do nothing. Because of this, in the parable the owner of the vineyard was called lazy and foolish. With that being said the question that needs to be asked is when should you start pulling weeds in your garden? The answer is quite simple, when you *see* the weeds. Oftentimes the work can be extremely taxing if one waits until the garden is overgrown with weeds. As soon as you see some form of break in communication, somehow, someway work should soon start to repair the communication lines. The longer you wait, the harder it will be to repair.

Now, what is not being said is that you and your partner should agree on every minor aspect of your thoughts, ideas or conversations. The earlier comment of, "When one person begins to see something slightly different than their partner and it is not understood or dealt with" may give the false impression that we should always agree with our partner in every thought and conversation. That is the furthest from the truth. What was actually meant in that statement was that when you see that you and your partner are beginning to see things differently, an attempt should be made to at least understand *why* we are seeing things differently. As soon as we see that we are perceiving things differently, we should at least attempt to understand why there is a difference in our perception. If at a bare minimum we understand *why* we are perceiving things differently, there is still a chance that we can have some form of effective dialogue. This dialogue will be able to exist because we are able to come to some form of common ground. This common ground or understanding of the way a person sees something will enable us to still communicate even though we may have a different understanding or dialect, per se, as opposed to a different language.

Just because we have a different way of viewing things, it doesn't necessarily mean that we have a different language or that we can't communicate. As long as we understand that we have a difference of opinion and then understand *why* we have that difference of opinion, it is still possible to communicate. When two people speak the same language but speak that same language differently, it is said that they have a different dialect not a different language. People with different dialects are still able to communicate because they understand that their words may differ in sound and meaning but not necessarily in definition. They also understand that they have a base and mutual understanding of their language. As long as we can concentrate on that base language and then get an understanding of why we see or say things differently, we may be able to look past our differences or dialects and will still be able to communicate effectively. Even though we may not agree on terms, we can communicate because of understanding. Let's first define dialect and then make sense of it with an example.

A dialect is: *A **regional** or **social variety** of a particular language* ***distinguished** by **pronunciation, grammar,** or **vocabulary***. According to the definition of a dialect, two people can have the same language, say the same sentence and because of some regional or **social** differences, the exact same sentence may mean something totally different to the two persons that are speaking. However because the two persons have a base knowledge of the language they're speaking and make an attempt to at least understand why they see things differently or understand each other's dialect, they are still able to communicate effectively. People may understand that the other person they are speaking to may be using pronunciation, grammar, or vocabulary totally different than they would because they are from a different regional or social environment. However, they can still make an *attempt* to understand the differences and will now be able to effectively communicate.

Let's look at an example. Someone may say, "That is a real cool cat." The first person, which we'll call Party A, may understand this to be that the cat being spoken of is a domesticated feline and since he is cool, that feline is not being subjugated to the heat at the moment. The second person or Party B being from a totally different regional or social sector may define this totally different. To party B a cat may be, metaphorically speaking, a gentleman that walks with poise, grace and confidence. Party B may also consider him to be cool because, again metaphorically, he seems to have the ability to remain calm, unstressed and maintain his composure even in heated situations thus earning the adjective, 'cool'.

The Meeting of Two Nations

Party A may not use the metaphors of Party B and possibly never will but because they have the same language and he at least attempts to understand why Party B uses these metaphors, they are still able to communicate. Party A understands that Party B is from a different region or social dynamic and therefore has a different dialect than he does. When one person has a different dialect from another person, all they need to do is exercise a little patience and understanding to realize *why* the other person may see things the way they see them and say things the way they say. This is how it is when two people come into being in a relationship. When they first come together they are from two totally different worlds (regions or social dynamics) and are actually two separate nations uniting. So you'll have two totally different people from two totally different households. They probably grew up with two totally different sets of rules, two totally different ways of doing things and they'll now expect their partner to agree totally on everything with them. Look at it from this angle. Think of two siblings that grew up with the same set of parents, in the same house, with the same set of rules, and the same way of doing things and they'll still have disagreements and arguments because they don't always see things the same way. If that is the case, it would be insane to think that two people from two totally different worlds would agree on everything and not have any disagreements. Yet, that is what we hope and strive for in relationships. What we have to see is that two people may speak the same language but because they may differ regionally, socially or even mentally, even if they grew up in the same house, they may have a different dialect. Because of this different dialect, more of an attempt to understanding the other person's view and less of an attempt to *push* your own beliefs or understandings on your partner will prove to be the most beneficial for healthy communication.

Now that was the process of creating effective communication with persons that have a different dialect but what if a couple have gotten to the point where they are speaking a different language? First of all, how do you even know if you are speaking a different language from your partner? You may both be speaking English or even Chinese for that matter and may not even realize that you are speaking a different language. Here is a litmus test to assist you in determining if you and your partner are speaking a different language. If you and your partner are frequently agitated while trying to express yourselves and constantly arguing when attempting to hold a conversation with one another, you may be speaking a different language. If you or your partner is more relaxed away from one another and more tense around each other, you are definitely speaking a different language. Something needs to be rectified before the same thing that happened at the tower of Babel happens to your relationship.

Remember, at the tower of Babel, some event took place and caused the people to all start speaking a different language and then something very important happened. This event is one of the greatest lessons that can be learned from this passage:

⁷ Go to, let us go down, and there **confound their language, that they may not understand one another**'s *speech.* ⁸ *So the* LORD **scattered them abroad** *from thence upon the face of all the earth: and they* **left off (or ceased) to build the city. Gen 11:7,8**

Once their language was confounded and they could no longer understand one another, they were scattered abroad or *separated.* They ceased to be productive in their great undertaking but again, more importantly, they separated. To get the full grasp of how this separation works a slow dissection of this passage needs to take place.

The Meeting of Two Nations

Here you have one people with one mind and one language. They are working productively for the greater good of the people as a whole. They are communicating their different ideas, thoughts, and concepts and bouncing them off of one another while still maintaining an industrious and positive working environment. When their language is confounded or changed and they can no longer communicate, you have to agree that some bewilderment and confusion must have begun to take place. Just think of it. Jim the architect is talking to Sally the builder and all is going well until BAM! For some strange reason they can no longer communicate. It would be my guess that they didn't just stop talking and then walked away from one another. No, I believe the process of their communication break is the same process that our communication break goes through. Jim and Sally are speaking one moment and the next moment they are looking at each other strange because they can't understand or believe what is coming out of the other person's mouth. They initially begin to slowly attempt to get the other person to understand what they are trying to say, to no avail. After a while they begin to get agitated and frustrated because what they are hearing isn't making any sense. They are even more frustrated because what they are saying isn't being understood. After agitation and frustration, anger will eventually take root and then resentment will soon grow. The resentment will come because one person will feel that they have these wonderful things inside of them that will help both of them if their partner would just try and understand. However, they feel that their partner isn't even trying to listen. It may not be that the person isn't trying; it may be that they can't.

People all over the world conduct business transactions on a continuous and daily basis. They may not speak the same language but they are still productive in their transactions. How do billions of people that speak totally different languages conduct business effectively even though they do not understand a word the other person is saying? The businesses will hire an interpreter that will translate all of their business goals, wants needs and desires and will also interpret what needs to be done to fulfill those wants, needs and desires. It may not be that parties don't want to fulfill these desires; it simply may be that they don't understand what is being requested of them to do. They may also be having a hard time getting the other person to understand what they need themselves. The translator's job is to correctly hear what is being said, decipher what is being said and then correctly translate it so that it is properly understood by the other party. The best translator is one that not only translates but one that will also teach one party's language to the other so that they may be able to communicate more independently. When dealing with Marriage, Family and Relationships, this translator is commonly referred to as a therapist.

Many people have stigmas about going to therapists. The reasons vary from family to family and from person to person. Some of the common reasons used or things said to justify not going to therapy are:

1. I don't want anyone in my business.
2. I don't want anyone in my head.
3. I don't want some outsider trying to tell me what I should be doing.
4. How can someone that doesn't know me tell me how to fix my problems?

I heard a gentleman say that he didn't believe in going to therapy because everyone he knew that went to therapy ended up divorced. Remember, a therapist is nothing more than a translator. At its core, the therapist is simply there to assist their clients in communicating. The therapist's job is to determine what language each person is speaking and then translate so the other person can understand and begin to communicate. So how can the gentleman make the claim that everyone he knew that went to therapy divorced? It's quite simple.

Usually what happens is that one person in the relationship sees that something is wrong and that they are unable to *properly* communicate. One party may suggest therapy and the other party will use one of the five excuses above not to go to therapy. The longer they wait, the larger the gulf of their miscommunication will become. As the gulf widens, so will agitation and frustration especially from the one partner that is trying to fix the issue. Remember what we said earlier that follows behind agitation and frustration, anger and resentment. It will be anger because you're not trying and resentment that you're leaving me alone to fix it. Once anger and resentment takes root, it will take some serious therapy to reverse these emotions. When resentment comes into play, the partner that is having these emotions begins to mentally pull away from the relationship and will often time cease in attempting to fix the issue. They have now determined that they want out of the relationship and there is almost nothing anyone can say or do that will change their mind. The party that was making the excuses about going to therapy begins to see this nonchalant attitude and out of fear of loss, express the desire to go to therapy. The other party may agree but will only be going through the motions because their mind has already been made up and hence, a lot of people that go to therapy get divorced. As in the story of the tower of

Babel, when the people began to speak different languages, the scattering or separation was inevitable without an interpreter. With an interpreter however, they could have continued with their great undertaking and even learned each other's language in order to tackle new obstacles that came their way.

One of the quickest ways to push your partner into speaking and hearing a different language is to begin speaking with negative connotations. We're advised not to do this in the book of Ephesians.

29Let no corrupt communication proceed out of your mouth, but that which is good to the use of edifying, that it may minister grace unto the hearers. **Ephesians 4:29**

This is saying that when we are communicating, our communication shouldn't be corrupt (of poor quality, bad, unfit for use, worthless). Instead we should be edifying (building up or building better than it was in its previous state) one another. This will give grace (joy, peace, delight) to those that we are speaking to. It should *never* be the desire of a person to tear down someone else with words.

Words should never be used to tear down. They should always be used to build up. Even if I am using words to assist someone in tearing down a negative image they may have of themselves, I will still have to use words to build the person up out of that rubble we just tore down. If you noticed, we tore down the negative image, not the person. If I have a thought in my mind and I want to bring it into fruition, I must use words to build it in the mind of others that will help me bring it into existence. If what is being said truly doesn't make sense to you, then either you skipped Chapter 3 or still don't understand *the purpose of marriage*. If you did read it, understood it but are unwilling to change then you have to question if you are truly ready to be married whether you are

118

married now or not. You must first understand the purpose of marriage so you can properly use your words to edify or they will eventually become corrupted and anything that becomes corrupted will eventually be destroyed.

Do I truly understand that when my spouse and I communicate it is the meeting of two foreign nations?

Can two foreign nations still communicate effectively?

What can I do to effectively communicate with my spouse?

~9~

Adultery is Never the Answer

Hosea 2:5, 7 NIV

Their mother has been unfaithful and has conceived them in disgrace. She said, 'I will go after my lovers, who give me my food and my water, my wool and my linen, my olive oil and my drink.'

She will chase after her lovers but not catch them; she will look for them but not find them. Then she will say, 'I will go back to my husband as at first, for then I was better off than now.'

Many people that may pick up this book may look through the table of contents and see a chapter on adultery and wonder why would I include a whole chapter on the subject in a marriage manual? I'm putting it in here because of the same reason that other manuals and handbooks put warnings in their books; because people are doing it, have done it or are thinking about doing it. You would think that it would be common sense for people to know not to spill liquids on their electronic equipment. However, consumers still get a warning page in the manual of the equipment they've recently purchased. It's not that consumers intentionally pour liquid onto their equipment. It's just that they don't see the danger in having their drinks or other liquids around their electronics. They *know* they will be careful around their equipment and because they *will* be careful, it will *not* happen to them. So, since they *are* being careful and it will *not* happen to them, they bring liquids around their equipment and then *accidentally* spill it onto their equipment thereby calling for the warning pages in the manuals.

One of the main causes for divorce is infidelity. It has been reported by clinical member of the American Association of Marital and Family Therapists (AAMFT) that almost 50% of all clients surveyed admitted to having an affair during some point of their relationship. In another study by Amato and Previti (2003), infidelity was the leading cause of divorces. Many theories have been applied to determining the growing cause of the epidemic like state of our modern relationships. Some attribute it to the fact that more women work outside of the home, usually working alongside male colleagues. Work brings people closer together and often times assist in the developing of relationships and bonding in order to have a productive and cohesive work environment. Another possible contributing factor is the greatness of modern technology. A person can now go online and *chat* with whomever they please. They can now chat with others which are often of the opposite sex and never have to leave the comfort of their homes. They can now do it without being under the scrutiny of some nosey neighbor, family member or church member. The emergence of the smart phone has also opened a new world of chat rooms, IM's, email, social games, social networks, text messages and anything else that may come out all at your fingertips in a moment's notice. I also may add right here that because a lot of these social conversations, virtual friendships and relationships are being developed while you are in the comfort of your own home, you tend to be more at ease than you normally would be and you're more apt to let your guard down a little further and a little sooner than you normally would. Because of all of these dynamics just mentioned, many people will be shocked to know that it is now easier for a woman to find herself in an adulterous relationship than a man. We'll let that sink in for a minute or two and explain it a little later on in the chapter.

So, just what is adultery or an affair? First of all you have to understand that adultery and an affair are both one in the same. An affair is just a euphemism that is used to describe adultery and is basically used as an attempt to make it more palatable than it really should be. At one time it was the person that was in or a person that was being affected by an adulterous relationship that used the term *affair*. It softened the blow and made the conversation a little more acceptable and pleasant. Adultery sounds more harsh, calculating and manipulative. Affair sounds lighter, inviting and a somewhat happy 'event' that just sort of happened. Regardless of whether it's called adultery or an affair, it is defined as when a married person is involved in an illegal relationship and intercourse is *always* involved. I know someone just got a dose of relief because they just thought, "Well, I'm good because I didn't sleep with anyone." Oh, contraire mon frère or mon soeur. Before you make that claim, you first have to define intercourse.

Intercourse - : a **connection** or dealings between persons or groups. 2: an **exchange** especially of **thoughts or feelings**. 3: **physical sexual contact** between individuals that involves the genitalia of at least one person.

According to the definition, intercourse is a connection first. It is an exchange of thoughts or feelings second and it is physical contact third. If this is the case, then adultery or the *affair* started long before sexual contact or even if the sexual encounter hasn't happened *yet*. Anyone that has ever found themselves in this position or know of someone that may have found themselves in this position would have to agree that long before the sexual encounter took place there was first a connection made and then eventually an exchange of thought or feelings. This brings us to understanding the two types of affairs. There is first the emotional affair and then there is the physical affair; both of which are totally different from the one night stand. A one night stand is a casual, no strings attached, sexual encounter that only happens that one time and the two parties are never to meet again. I have to say right here that the one night stand is equally as wrong as the affair and just as dangerous. It is still very possible to lose your family over a onetime encounter. Having a habit of one night stands is a separate matter unto itself. It is sure to get someone found out as well as lose everything you would as if you were in affair. However, what is being discussed now is the development of an outside relationship which challenges the very foundation of the marital relationship you are already in.

Let's get back to our definition of intercourse, which we now agree, that is always a part of adultery or an affair. Remember we said that intercourse is a *connection*, an *exchange of thoughts or feelings* and *finally physical, sexual contact*. If this is the case, then let's look at it from this angle. A married person works for the 'Noname' Corporation. The married person has been placed on a new and maybe stressful project with a new partner. The new work partner makes the transition smooth and painless and the two colleagues click. Because they click, they talk often and find out that they have similar interest and begin to talk even more. This so called clicking we just described is the actual *connection* being developed between the two coworkers. Since they have a connection, they tend to talk even more and will soon begin to look forward to seeing or at least hearing from their new found comrade. The coworkers will even begin to look at each other as friends now. They will begin to send quick text messages and email reminders for upcoming meetings and events. They will even begin to send jokes and funny stories because their friend *will love to hear this one*. They begin to bounce ideas off of one another, get advice and even begin to exchange thoughts. Eventually, they will express their mutual respect and express how much they enjoy each other's company, friendship, and gratitude for just being there when they really needed them. The text messaging, emails and phone calls may become more frequent as time goes on and a quick thought of wondering what the other person is doing may even begin to cross their minds.

I have to stop right here to admit that the scenario just described may *seem* totally innocent because no one has physically crossed any lines *yet*. However, if **<u>any</u> part (and I do mean <u>any</u> part)** of this scenario is *intentionally* being kept away from the knowledge of a spouse, then you have already slipped into an extremely, dark grey area and are already in or developing an emotional affair and don't even realize it. Here is where things have the tendency to get real slippery and dangerous. Here is where we'll have a conversation with ourselves and begin to justify our actions of what we have done, what we are doing or what we will do. In one instance we'll tell ourselves, *I am developing a very cohesive and productive relationship with a colleague that I respect immensely.* In another instance we'll say, *I am beginning to look forward to hearing from or seeing my colleague more and more. There is nothing wrong with that because we have a lot to talk about and we really enjoy each other's company and conversations. Even though my colleague is attractive, I don't really find them attractive because we're* **just** *friends.*

Again, all of this can be *perceived* as innocent and people find themselves in this situation on a daily basis. To be honest, at this point, you aren't *really* doing anything wrong other than giving someone other than your spouse more time in your life and your mind than you should. At this juncture, you're just standing at the edge of the sea or the edge of the cliff of adultery *gazing,* yet in the darkness of your mind, contemplating the leap.

I say sea or cliff because if you leap and no one finds out, you are at the sea. You can take a dip, enjoy your swim, dry off as best you can, lie about how your clothes got wet and go back to where you came from unbeknownst to anyone else. If you're found out however, you've just stepped off of a cliff and are sure to lose life or limb; you will either lose your life itself, the life of your marriage or the limb of trust that you've been growing since you and your spouse first met.

Thankfully at this point however, none of this has transpired. Right now you are still on solid ground. All you've done is spent a little more time than you should with someone other than your spouse. However, you begin to tell yourself, *No one has really said anything out of the way; only an off color joke or a comment that would be a little too risqué to be said in front of my spouse. Other than that, I am still on solid ground and I'm in full control of the situation.* That is what we tell ourselves. The sad truth however, is that we are standing at the very edge of danger and don't even know it. We are one decision away from possibly losing everything we have worked so hard for.

The above situation happens pretty much the same way for both men and women with minor differences. Men, on one hand, usually sees what's going on in the friendship a tad bit earlier than women and may stick around just to see how far they can look over the cliff without actually falling off of the cliff. Men will play mind games on themselves and try to convince themselves that, "Nah, she doesn't really look at me that way so I can look over without falling off". Women, on the other hand, also attempt to play mind games on themselves but they try to convince themselves that there may not really be a cliff. They'll tell themselves, "We're only friends so there can't be a cliff", so they attempt to get as close to the edge of the cliff as possible without actually falling over. The thrill for men is getting right over the edge without falling off and the thrill for women is getting as close as possible without falling off. What both fail to realize is that the edge of the cliff is just that, the edge of the cliff. One missed step and you might as well yell "Geronimo" because you're going over.

The next thing I'm about to say is the most crucial part of this entire chapter. If you didn't read anything before this part or you close the book after this part, it will be fine with me and I pray all goes well with you but please slow down, read and understand the very next sentence. *The very second you express feelings for someone other than your spouse and the other person reciprocates, you have just fallen over the cliff. You have just entered into adultery, an illegal relationship or an affair.* Intercourse has been committed and it is only a matter of time before what is now verbal and emotional becomes overpowering and physical. Because this subject is so broad and in depth, there isn't enough room to go into it in its entirety in this book. However, if you have the slightest hint of conviction after reading this, it is my serious recommendation that you look up Emotional and Physical Affairs and become acquainted with the signs and see how one can lead to the other. Your studies will also share how to come out of such a relationship.

Now, we've talked about the definition of adultery and we've talked about how people find themselves in this type of relationship but we've also made the claim that it is easier for women to find themselves in this type of relationship more so than men. Why is that? For the longest our society wanted us to believe that women were not as sexual as men. It wasn't until recently that society has begun to believe that women look at men as often, if not more often, than men look at women. Even with these new understandings, in the back of our minds, we still somehow believe that women aren't as sexual as men. The most detrimental part of this whole scenario is that women made an attempt to believe the same thing about their own sexuality. Even though women *know* what they are thinking in their minds and how they feel about their sexuality, they still fall into the trap of believing the dogma that has been spread throughout society. Most women believe that there are *good* girls and *bad* girls and want others to perceive them as *good* girls (Langley, 2005). They believe that any woman that does anything outside of what society says, *is* the bad girl. The truth of the matter is that there is no such thing as good girls or bad girls. There are just women that have their own sexuality. Because women themselves believed this erroneous information that there is such a thing as a good girl or a bad girl, many women go into the world unprepared for what most men already know awaits them, the possibility of an affair.

Let's look at it from this angle. Men and women tend to walk through jungles differently. Men, for the most part, walk through the jungle knowing and understanding that there is danger but they also understand that there is something called quicksand. Men understand that quicksand may look like solid ground on the surface but also has the ability to bog a person down and suffocate them. They know that with quicksand this can happen before they even realize that the ground they started walking on isn't as solid as they thought. Women, on the other hand, know the dangers of the jungle as well but may not have the slightest inkling of what quicksand is. They may be walking along on the lookout for obvious danger and then all of a sudden feel the ground become sloshy under their feet. They may get up to their knees in mud and think, *this is different.* They may get up to their waist or chest in mud and think, "There is no way possible that I will do much worse than I'm doing right now." However, by the time the mud and sand is up to their neck and is about to go into their mouths is when they realize they have no control of the situation and have sunk lower than they ever intended to go.

This is why it is much easier for women to fall into this type of relationship. Many women feel that only bad girls have affairs, commit adultery or have intercourse with men other than their husbands. This is the furthest from the truth. The absolute truth is that most women want to feel beautiful; they want to feel beautiful for themselves and want to be seen as beautiful by others. The greatest secret that is hidden right in the open is that most women *want* to be desired by other men. It's not that they necessarily want to *be* with other men as much as they want to be noticed by other men and other women for that matter. Some women may want to refute this at the onset and it's alright but this is the very reason that women spend so much time in the mirror getting their hair and makeup impeccable before they leave. It's the same reason they'll change their outfits several times before they deem it perfect and it's also the reason that they'll look at themselves in a full length mirror from every possible angle before leaving the house. If you're a young lady and this doesn't apply to you, then I apologize. I wasn't talking about you. I was talking about every other woman that does this. If you're a man and you realize your lady does this, don't be alarmed. This is no different than when you suck in your gut and look at yourself in the mirror. We are all a little vain to some degree or another but the women's scales tend to slide a little heavier in this area.

It is the woman's *desire* to feel desired and her possible lack of understanding of her own sexuality is what makes it easier for her to fall into an illegal type of relationship. Her misinformed images of 'good' girls and 'bad' girls and her lack of knowledge of the dangers of the quicksand do not work in her favor either. All of today's technologies, social networks and gadgets only compounds the problem and makes the slippery slope even slipperier than before.

Now two of the most important questions people ask concerning this subject are 1) why do people commit adultery and 2) how do you come out of it? To answer these two questions, we'll look at Gomer, the wife of the prophet Hosea. Before we go any further it must be said that even though we are using Gomer, a woman, in our example of why people find themselves in these types of relationships, the reasons are exactly the same for men as well. In Hosea 2:5 it says:

5 Their mother has been unfaithful and has conceived them in disgrace. She said, **'I will go after my lovers, who give me my food and my water, my wool and my linen, my olive oil and my drink.'** *Hosea 2:5 NIV*

Hosea, the husband of Gomer, was not only a man of God but also a prophet of God. This means that God not only loved Hosea but He also trusted him to tell the people what He was saying. In order for God to trust Hosea, he had to be a good man. So we can't say that Gomer's problem was with Hosea. The problem ultimately lay in Gomer herself. In Verse 5, Gomer said that she was going to chase after her lovers (plural) and these lovers were going to give her food, water, wool, linen, oil and drink. These things represent everything she wanted and possibly everything she needed. So in actuality, Gomer was feeling a lack or void in her life. She felt that there was something she wasn't getting or something she was missing while married to Hosea. These are things she felt that outsiders could provide for her better than her husband could. In this instance, Hosea could also represent a woman; she could be a devoted wife and stay at home mom that kept the house impeccable. If Gomer was a man, he could feel that there was something he was missing even though his spouse gave him everything he needed; maybe not everything he wanted but at least everything he needed.

Regardless of who represents the male and who represents the female, it is not the spouse that is being cheated on that has the issue. It is the spouse that will go after other lovers that feels that something is missing. There is nothing that their spouse can say or do to fill that void they are feeling. They themselves, their attitudes and their outlook on life are the only things that can fill that *perceived* emptiness they have in their lives. Much like Gomer, people will step out of their marriage when they feel they are not getting a need met or feel they are not getting something they deserve. In many cases, like Gomer's, that was the furthest from the truth. She finally realized that she was actually getting what she needed from her husband because she eventually said:

7 She will chase after her lovers but not catch them; she will look for them but not find them. Then she will say, **'I will go back to my husband as at first, for then I was better off than now.'** *Hosea 2:7 NIV*

She may not have been getting *everything* she *wanted* but she was getting *everything* she *needed* as she soon realized. When Gomer chased after her lovers, she like most men and women are looking for that possible 20 to 25% that their spouse isn't giving them in the marriage. Like Gomer, they leave the 75 to 80% behind thinking what they are chasing will give them an eternal 100%.

This chase usually falls in one of two categories. It will either fall in what I call the 'Used Car Syndrome' or the 'Joy Ride'. In the 'Used Car Syndrome', a person owns a decent and dependable running car but the paint has lost some of its luster and the car may now have a couple of dings in it. Instead of working with what you have, you go to the nearest car lot and *fall in love* with this *new* shiny car. You find it hard to believe that no one bought or appreciates this car. You throw caution to the wind and buy it because this car has *everything* that you've been missing. It's a little more expensive but it's alright because *it has everything* that you've been missing. What you don't realize is that just because that car is new *to you*, it was driven by someone else before and that is why it's on the lot *looking* for a new owner. This car, even though it has a shiny new paint job also has a slipping transmission and a sputtering engine. It doesn't always work like it should but by the time you realize it, it's too late. You've already purchased the *new* car and already have it at your house. It actually has more problems than it is worth and now you want your old dependable car back. Usually one of three things happens at this point. First, you stay with that shiny broke car because you are too embarrassed to admit you made a mistake. You practically gave your dependable car away so that you could go buy a lemon and now you feel stuck. The second thing is you try to go back and buy your old dependable car only to find out that it will now cost you more than it did before or thirdly, you find out that someone else has already bought your dependable car. They appreciate it so much more than you did. They knocked the dings out, gave it a new paint job and now have it looking so much better than you ever did. Many people waste years chasing after that 100% or that *shiny new car*. They go from husband to husband, from wife to wife, from husband to different man and from wife to all sorts of women.

They are seeking something they will never find. They are trying to catch a vapor with their bare hands and usually become more delusional as time goes on. The entire summation of this chapter, along with the explanation will be told in the last 5 sentences of this paragraph. If you understand these last 5 sentences, you are well on your way to success. Aren't you glad you picked up this book? You'll save yourself years of heartache and pain if you understand the very next few sentences. Here we go. First, that 100% you are looking for *does not exist*. 100% would allude to your spouse being perfect and there is only one perfect being. After that, there is no other, so get that out of your mind. Secondly, there is *no* such thing as a soul mate. Yes, as time goes on and our souls intertwine, they *can* become mates and that is beautiful. However, that other thing we are thinking about only happens in romance novels and does not exist in reality.

The second category for the reasons of an affair is called 'The Joy Ride'. It's true that if a couple stays married long enough they tend to get comfortable with one another. Getting comfortable in a relationship has its pros as well as its cons. One benefit of getting comfortable in a relationship is you don't have to work as hard as you use to. You get to know their likes and dislikes. You've learned what you have to do to make them happy and you have a pretty good idea of what will cause them to get upset. In this instance, the pro is the con as well. Now that you are too comfortable with your spouse you *won't* put in as much effort as you use to. Since there is a lack of effort, the relationship may take on a carefree or even lackadaisical feel. The security and even the dependability that were once appreciated in the relationship have now become stale, dull and predictable. The relationship that was once so exiting has now become mundane. This staleness, lack of excitement and predictability can all be summed up with one word, boring! People want fun, excitement and some even feel the need for spontaneity. If a person finds themselves bored in his or her marriage, another person outside of their marriage may provide that needed excitement. They could now find themselves confused between what is secure and dependable and what is exhilarating and exciting.

Let's look at someone with a dependable car again. A person can have a very dependable car but it lacks flash and thrill. They may go test drive a motorcycle just for the *fun* of it. *OMG! It was awesome*, you tell yourself. *I felt free, uninhibited and young again. The danger and the vibration of the engine just did something to me.* You throw caution to the wind and buy the motorcycle. You're smarter than *most* people so you don't get rid of your car. No, you want to keep both if you can get away with it. You have the best of both worlds. You have the dependability of your *old faithful car* and now you have the excitement of your motorcycle. This would be fine if you were dealing with vehicles but in this instance you're actually dealing with people. Because you are dealing with people, unbeknownst to yourself, you will begin to spend more time with one person than the other. You won't even realize it yourself. As human nature would have it, because the motorcycle is the object that is giving you pleasure, you will begin to neglect the object that is giving you security. When the dependable car breaks down because of your lack of *maintenance*, you will now be stuck with what has been giving you pleasure.

This will bother you somewhat in the beginning because you were simply *use* to the dependability of the car. Reality won't *really* set in until life becomes uncomfortable. When it is ice cold outside and the rain is beating on you or it is now hot as Hades, you may actually come to regret your test drive on the motorcycle.

As stated earlier, the 365 day a year of romance and excitement only happens in romance novels and movies. As a matter of fact, it doesn't even happen in Hollywood. If you notice it's at the end of the movie that people fall in love and get married. We tend to think that what we are seeing is the sum total of their lives because the movie is over. No, the movie is over but their new life together is just beginning. It is a strong possibility that they will *not make* it. It's an even stronger possibility that you won't make it either unless you and your spouse grasp or understand the principles being taught in this book.

Remember, this isn't Hollywood and our life isn't written in some script. Our lives are unfolded like the petals of a delicate flower. Every decision we make either unfolds or stifles another petal. No matter what issues we may have with the unfolding of our petals, adultery will *never* be the answer. Many people think they will find that one thing they are missing in their lives with an affair. They also believe they can recapture the excitement of their youth with the thrills of one. This may be true in the beginning because the people caught up in an adulterous relationship don't have a *real* life together. They are living in a fantasy. Like all fantasies, everything is grand. There are no bills, mortgages, children, insurance or anything else for that matter to discuss. A fantasy life is full of fun and excitement.

When *real* life joins the fantasy, the fantasy has met its demise. The same pitfalls and problems encountered in the legal relationship will be the same in the adulterous relationship. However, now the problems will be multiplied because the affair has no base. Its very foundation is built upon lies, distrust and deceit. Even after reading this, some will attempt to make an adulterous relationship work. I'm not saying that it can't work but let's just say you do attempt to make your affair work. You leave your spouse for your lover and now *real* life sets in. You will *never* be totally relaxed and fully trusting in that relationship. If a few moments in the day isn't accounted for, or your new lover is sending text messages or emails, suspicion and guilt will eat away at your very insides. Suspicion will begin to take small but continuous bites out of you. You will begin to constantly wonder if your new lover is doing what was done to your or their jilted spouse. Guilt will soon be a greater burden to bear than suspicion. It will be because you know, somewhere in the back of your mind, no matter how good you feel about your new situation, *you reap what you sow.* You will begin to feel that you deserve whatever you get. You will almost come to expect it. You will live with that fear and constant pressure until what you fear happens or until you aren't able to take the pressure anymore. You will eventually choose to leave that relationship for the sake of your own sanity.

If you are that unhappy in your marriage, attempt to get some help so that you and your spouse may begin to speak the same language. Try everything you can to repair what damage that has been done. Even if the issues aren't your fault, attempt to save the business you said you would invest your all into. Don't let your attempts be halfhearted just to say you checked the box and can now say, "Well, I tried." Take ownership of your marriage. Even if your spouse isn't putting forth as much effort as you would like, you be the superhero your marriage needs. No, I can't guarantee that this will work. What I can guarantee is that you will never be able to fix your own house by spending time at someone else's. I can also guarantee you will never be able to fix someone else's house because the tools you possess rightfully belong to those in your own home.

Do I truly understand when I'm beginning to approach the quicksand and its catastrophic dangers?

Do I understand the 'new' used car is never 'truly' brand new and that 'joy ride' is not always a joy?

~10~

The Conclusion of the Matter

Ecclesiastes 12:9-11

⁹ *Not only was the Teacher wise, but he also imparted knowledge to the people. He pondered and searched out and set in order many proverbs.* ¹⁰ *The Teacher searched to find just the right words, and what he wrote was upright and true.* ¹¹ *The words of the wise are like goads, their collected sayings like firmly embedded nails—given by one shepherd.*

The book of Ecclesiastes was written by a very wise man. It's safe to say that much of his wisdom came from his God given gifts and talents but if you ever read Ecclesiastes, you'll be able to see that much of his wisdom also came from many life experiences. If I was a betting man, I would bet that not only did he learn from his own life experiences but he also learned from the life experiences of others. A wise man is one that *learns* from his experiences and puts those experiences into practice. The wisest of men however is one that learns from the experiences of others. I have been told that, especially for my youth, I am a wise man but I also continue to strive to be among the wisest of men (learning from the experience of others). You don't always have to hit your head on the brick wall to see how hard it actually is. I've seen too many people hit their heads and I know exactly how hard the wall is. I don't need bruises to prove it.

As a man that has been *happily* (notice what I said; happily) married to the same woman for almost 20 years without any type of separation, I can honestly say that over the years I've learned some things. I've intensely studied and still continue to study people and why they do what they do. I've even continued my education, gearing it towards the understanding and betterment of marriage, relationships and family. I've read countless books, articles and essays all for a single purpose; so that I can assist others in not only being successful in their marriages and relationships but also be happy while in them. A lot of people are successful in making their marriages work but the question has to be asked, *are they happy*? Seeing people happy in their relationships and with their family is one of my greatest desires. Sometimes while I'm walking through my house or while I'm shaving and looking at myself in the mirror I would often think and say to myself, "Man, I wish everyone could find and have the level of peace and happiness that I've found."

My studies have been very rewarding for my research. Many things have also been revealed to me because of my experiences and my studies. Referring back to verses 10 and 11 of Ecclesiastes, it says:

[10] *The Teacher **searched** to find **just the right words**, and what he wrote was **upright and true**.*[11] *The **words of the wise are like goads**, their collected sayings like firmly embedded nails—given by one shepherd.*

I'm not trying to put myself in the same category of the teacher in any way, shape or form. What I can say is that I've attempted to travel the same roads as he. That particular teacher searched for just the right words. It also says that what he wrote was upright and true. The

140

question has to be asked, why did the teacher search to find *just the right words*? Apparently the teacher has learned some great lessons during his lifetime. Obviously, since he wrote them down, he wanted others to benefit from the lessons he learned. He had to search for just the right words to first, draw the people in. Then they may actually want to read his words and possibly seek correction. He next had to make his correction palatable and easy to receive. The teacher then uses a very distinct idiom to describe his own words. He uses the word '*goads*'. A goad is a long stick used to *prod or urge an animal* into a certain direction. When dealing with people, the goad is used to *provoke or stimulate* an individual into a new level of thinking and eventually living.

Because of the use of this word 'goad', chapter 1, Come Let Us Reason Together, and Chapter 2, Know Thyself, had to be included in this book. If we remember, Chapter 1 introduces us to the fact that many of our relationship mishaps have been self inflicted due to poor decisions that stem from our own bad habits and possible bad information. Chapter 2 showed us that we have many of these bad habits and make these bad decisions because we don't truly understand who we are. It shows us how we make many of our decision based on appetite and it's that same appetite that makes *all other animals 'react' instinctively* to situations they may find themselves in. The first 2 chapters are must reads before any other chapters. If you don't read those first, you will only be receiving a part of what is actually being taught. Reading this book without reading Chapters 1 and 2 will be like someone giving you keys to a brand new car and you not reading the manual on how to start the car. All of your life you've been using keys to start cars but with this car the keys are only to open the glove compartment. Now you'll be frustrated because you have this brand new vehicle, and you thought you could operate it like the things you had before. It doesn't work that way. Just like you can't put new wine in old wine skins, you can't put new thoughts and ideas in old mindsets.

Chapters 3 and 4, the Purpose and Courting chapters, are the precursors to marriage. Those two chapters are designed for those who are not yet married however; they are still beneficial to those who are married. It may clear up some false perceptions of what you have of marriage. These false opinions may be what is keeping you bound and frustrated. Chapter 5, the Love section, is good as a precursor also but also begins to mesh with the sections for persons that are already married. It teaches the true meaning of love and not this watered down, base level of a thing that we have come to call love. If poor communication cripples a relationship, then this thing that we call love has tied a plastic bag over its head. Chapter 6 through 9 are mainly to assist those that are already married but is a great tool and preconditioning for those that are yet to be married. The entire book will be a help for anyone that is divorced. It may show where possible wrong turns were made in the previous marriage as well as offer alternatives.

The simple fact that you picked up and read this book proves that you have the greatest desire to have a successful and happy marriage. It shows that you view your marriage certificate as more than just a piece of paper. It also shows that you are so serious about being successful and happy in your relationship, that you are willing to learn a different way of doing things. It proves that you are also willing to change the way you have been doing them. Yes, getting knowledge is great but understanding is better, however, wisdom comes from implementation and application. That's why James 1:22 says:

The Conclusion of the Matter

*But be ye **doers** of the **word**, and not hearers only, deceiving your own selves.*
James 1:22

That's exactly what happens when we hear something that we know to be true and still fail to have our lives transformed by that truth. We deceive ourselves because we justify our slackness within our own thoughts. So take what you have read, meditate on it and then be *fruitful and multiply* in the truest sense of that formula. If you don't fully understand what was just said, I suggest you read this book one more time as you have missed some extremely important points. I pray for your attainment of Knowledge and Understanding since we now know better. I pray for implementation and application of what you have learned because that will lead to a true manifestation of Wisdom. I pray most of all, for Peace and Blessings over the life of you, your marriage and your family.

Your Friend and Brother,

C. Joseph Simpson

Epilogue

Very few people get married with the goal of being miserable, making their spouse miserable and ending up divorced. Most people get married with the very best intentions. They have the grandest ideas of what a marriage is and how their partner should be and act *after* they are married. They step in with their best foot forward intending to make this marriage work. They feel that the sky is the limit and that all things are possible after they say, "I do."

Slowly, the bright colors of life begins to fade into a dismal grey and the once optimist gradually becomes a pessimist. I've seen this gradual progression range from a few days of being married to being married for decades. This progression of falling away usually follows the same path every time. First, we stop being the right person. Next, we forget the basics and then we take our eyes off of the prize.

A successful marriage takes two things; you have to find the right person but most importantly, you have to be the right person. All too often we focus on finding the right person and forget about being the right person. That is called being selfish. At the end of a warm conversation or heated argument (whatever you want to call it), take *all* of your emotions out of the equation and ask yourself one simple and *honest* question. *Was I being selfish?* If your answer is no, wait until the following morning and ask yourself again. The trick is to take your partner completely out of the scenario and focus totally on you. I guarantee you'll find traces of selfishness in there.

This book in its entirety is all about the basics. It's all about what Mom and Dad should have taught you but maybe just didn't get around to. It would be a total waste of time for someone to read this book to see what their spouse should be doing. This book is for the benefit of the reader. Since you are the reader, it's all about you and what *you* should be doing and understanding. If you want your spouse or future spouse to get a different understanding of marriage, then have them read the book also or even with you. During your reading, discuss your portion of the book as it pertains to you. After a chapter is read, let the husband or future husband discuss his understandings before he read the chapter and his understandings *after* he read the chapter. The crucial point is for him to discuss what he needs to change about *himself* to bring his new understanding into fruition. The young lady needs to do the exact same thing afterwards. This will ensure that there is a correct understanding of the basics and a plan to get you there.

The last step of falling away is taking our eyes off of the prize. To help you with that, I'm going to give you an example I was given and then the best advice I ever received. My mother told me that two days into their marriage, back in 1956, my father came to her and said, "Say *divorce*." She said, "What?" He said, "Say the word *divorce*." My mother said, "I'm not saying that!" He said, "Just say the word please." She said, "Ok, divorce." My father then said, "Good. You said it. Now, I don't ever want to hear *that* word in *this* house again". Basically he was saying that divorce was not an option; we're going to have to work through whatever issues that may come up. They were married for almost 30 years before my father passed away.

Now, the best advice I ever received came from my aunt and uncle, my father's baby brother. I am forever grateful. Two weeks before I got married, nearly 20 years ago, they sat my wife and I down at their kitchen table and said with that deep Southwest Louisiana accent, "You see these people that have been married for 20, 30, 40 and even 50 years, don't *ever* think that they didn't go through *something*. They just *decided* to work through it. You are no different from them and they are no different from you." They have been married for 50 years and are still pushing strong.

My beloved family, it is possible to have the best and most productive marriage you have ever dreamed of. Not only can you have it but more importantly you can be happy while in it. The only things that are keeping you from such an enjoyment are you, your understanding and your willingness to change.

About the Author

C. Joseph Simpson is a native of Lafayette, LA. He grew up the youngest of five children. After his father passed away, his mother remarried and then he became the youngest of ten children from his now blended family. He received his Bachelor's degree from Southern University in Baton Rouge, LA and has geared his education to Marital and Family Therapy. He is a member of the American Association for Marriage and Family Therapy and the Georgia Christian Counselors Association.

C. Joseph Simpson is a licensed minister at Faith Outreach Christian Life Center located in the suburbs of Augusta, GA. He currently serves as an associate minister but has served in the capacity of Pastor's Assistant, Teen Pastor, Teen Advocate, Spiritual Advisor and mentor to many of the congregation's parishioners and those of the local community.

His over 18 years of military service has afforded him the opportunity to study, speak to and advise couples and families all over the world of all different races and nationalities on the basic principles of marriage and family.

Mr. Simpson has been found teaching these principles at churches, civic and social organizations, prisons, shelters, small group meetings and one on one. His motto is, "Where there is a need, there shall I be."

He has been happily married to Cynthia M. Simpson of Baton Rouge, LA for nearly 20 years. They have four children, Trey, Jabril, Josiah and Jaelah.

References:

Amato, P.R., & Previti, D. (2003. People's reasons for divorcing: Gender, social class, the life course, and adjustment. Journal of Family Issues. 24, 602-626

Langley, Michelle. Women's infidelity : living in limbo : what women really mean when they say, "I'm not happy. St. Louis, Mo: McCarlan Pub, 2005.